WITHDRAWN

Maplewood

# HOW TO WRITE YOUR COLLEGE APPLICATION ESSAY

Kenneth A. Nourse

**VGM Career Horizons**
*NTC/Contemporary Publishing Group*

**Library of Congress Cataloging-in-Publication Data**

Nourse, Kenneth A.
    How to write your college application essay / by Kenneth A. Nourse.
       p.    cm. — (VGM opportunities series)
    ISBN 0-8442-4169-5
      1. College applications—United States.    2. Exposition (Rhetoric).
3. Universities and colleges—United States—Admission.   I. Title.
II. Series.
LB2351.52.U6N68
378.1'056—dc20                               92-37909
                                                CIP

Published by VGM Career Horizons
A division of NTC/Contemporary Publishing Group, Inc.
4255 West Touhy Avenue, Lincolnwood (Chicago), Illinois 60712-1975 U.S.A.
Copyright © 1994 by NTC/Contemporary Publishing Group, Inc.
All rights reserved. No part of this book may be reproduced, stored in a retrieval
system, or transmitted in any form or by any means, electronic, mechanical,
photocopying, recording, or otherwise, without the prior written permission of
NTC/Contemporary Publishing Group, Inc.
Printed in the United States of America
International Standard Book Number: 0-8442-4169-5

99 00 01 02 03 04 ML 22 21 20 19 18 17 16 15 14 13 12 11 10 9 8 7 6 5

# Contents

About the Author   v
Acknowledgments   vii
Introduction   ix

**1** **Why Colleges Require an Application Essay   1**
Getting to Know You   2
Avoiding the Guessing Game   2
Standing Out in the Crowd   3
Conditioning Your Mind   3

**2** **The Essay as an Application Component   6**
Orderliness   7
Originality   8

**3** **How Much the Essay Counts   10**

**4** **What an Application Essay Is   13**
Defining an Essay   14
Expressing Yourself   14
Keeping Your Essay Brief   16
Elements of an Essay   16
The Range of Topics   18

**5** **Choosing Your Topic   21**
Thinking About Your Options   22
Preparing Yourself   23
A Sample Essay   24

**6 Getting Psyched 28**
Avoiding Procrastination 29
How to Make an Outline 29
Building Self-Esteem 31
Be Yourself 32

**7 The Ultimate Crutch: The
Five-Paragraph Theme 36**

**8 Proofreading Your Essay 39**

**9 A Potpourri of Essays 41**

**10 The Ultimate Falsehood 61**

**11 What the Pros Think 70**

**Appendix—Advisories 93**
**Afterword—Communicating
Clearly 95**

# About the Author

Kenneth A. Nourse received his A.B. in English from Middlebury College in 1952. After brief experiences as a newspaper reporter and a radio announcer, he began a career in college admissions which was to last 33 years, interrupted by a five-year stint in public relations/fund raising/alumni relations at his alma mater. Other colleges he served include Clarkson University, Rochester Institute of Technology, Worcester Polytechnic Institute, and Union (New York) College.

In 1965, he participated in the African Scholarship Program of American Universities (ASPAU), interviewing candidates in what was then known as British West Africa (Nigeria, West Cameroon, Ghana, Guinea, Liberia, Gambia).

He is a past president of the New England Association of College Admissions Counselors and, upon his retirement in June 1991, he was awarded the Distinguished Service

A01622409

Award of the New York State Association of College Admissions Counselors. He is a cofounder and president of Fitzwilliam Associates, Ltd., an admissions consulting firm. He is currently a member of the Board of Overseers of Middlebury College.

## ACKNOWLEDGMENTS

Admissions Staff, Carnegie-Mellon University

Admissions Staff, Lake Forest College

Admissions Staff, Union College

Dr. William F. Elliott, Carnegie-Mellon University

Francis B. Gummere, Lake Forest College

Alan B. Crocker, St. Mark's School (Massachusetts)

Ina Miller, educational consultant

All those quoted

Unidentified student authors

William Noble, Cornwall, Vermont

# Introduction

This book provides assistance to young men and women who are about to apply to colleges which require an essay as part of the application process. The author assumes that readers are, at most, intimidated, or, at least, uncomfortable with such a task and attempts to overcome individual fears by restoring confidence and causing natural abilities to surface.

Colleges require the essay because it is the easiest way to find out what makes you "tick." They like the way in which it offers each applicant the opportunity to reveal their personna; to exercise their imagination; to draw upon their experience; to parade their grammatical skills; to use an appropriate vocabulary; and, to make whatever point they wish.

As you read through *How to Write Your College Application Essay,* you will begin to understand the essay requirement and feel better about it. The chapters on the essay as a component and how much it counts are fairly subjective. We could probably argue about them. By now, you should know what an essay is but some time is spent in exploration. Choosing a topic requires some time and thought. It may prove to be the most difficult part of the whole exercise. Once you decide on a topic, things become much easier for you. There is a full chapter devoted to getting you in the right frame of mind to do your writing. If you can get yourself properly psyched, you will watch the words "roll" off your pen. The chapter on the "Ultimate Crutch" is good discipline and goes beyond essay writing to the roots of how you think and express yourself; give it some respect. When it comes time to proofread it should be done with great care because proofreading represents an attitudinal approach which, when extrapolated upon, reveals many things about you as a person. The several examples of student essays will give you many ideas for topics and approaches. The professional observations are intended to share with you the experience and knowledge of some people who have been reading college application essays for many years. The pros do have some very good advice for you and you would be well-advised to pay attention. The advisories are self-explanatory and are meant to be carried through life.

In summary, the author is suggesting that you have more ability than you think and writing the essay is the time for you to prove yourself through written expression. You will have a great deal of support all around you. Even the admissions officers are rooting for you to do a bangup job. All you have to do is pick a topic, think it through, make your outline, and write the essay. If the finished product sounds like you, and you like the way it reads, it will probably be an impressive essay.

# Why Colleges Require an Application Essay 1

"Ask any high school senior what the worst part of applying for college is, and you'll hear one answer: the essay. What can have the most beneficial results for many students causes the most pain and anguish. Why? Because students have to put themselves on the line with the personal essay . . . Students are the topic of the exercise."

So writes Susan K. Biemeret, college consultant at Adlai Stevenson High School in Prairie View, Illinois, in a recent issue of the *Pioneer Press.*

She is absolutely right. Most applicants to college are not comfortable with writing essays, and many cannot understand why colleges insist upon requiring such a writing sample. The thinking is that if colleges have so many applications on file, then having to read all of the essays is just a great deal of extra work. It would seem prudent for colleges to save themselves a good deal of time and aggravation by simply doing away with the requirement.

## Getting to Know You

Unfortunately for applicants, colleges do not see it this way. On the contrary, they feel that an essay is a very good way to assess the subjective side of a candidate—all those good things that transcend GPAs, SATs, and class ranks. What kinds of things are we talking about specifically? Things like your ability to think critically and creatively, your ability to communicate your feelings, a peek at your value system and sense of humor—in short, the real you.

An essay gives colleges an opportunity to make several judgments relating to the way you think and just how adept you are at translating those thoughts onto paper. Some of the more obvious judgment calls focus on the strength of your vocabulary, your ability to use and manipulate words, how you develop your thoughts, how your thinking translates through the written word, how well you spell, your ability to use proper grammar, whether and how well you proof your work. Much of the college experience deals with ideas and creative thinking. If students are to be full participants in this kind of stimulating activity, then they must have the ability to communicate their ideas on paper in a way that can be understood by any reader.

## Avoiding the Guessing Game

One of the games many applicants play as they approach the task of writing college essays is trying to guess the essay response a college wants. This is a serious mistake that you should try hard to avoid. Colleges offer topics upon which to write either because they think you need help in finding a topic or because they believe their assigned topic might produce a more intellectual response. Basically, colleges are trying to find out if you think, how you think, and what the written result of your thinking is. If you spend time trying to figure out what colleges want you to spew back, the thrust of the exercise is defeated. Forget about trying to guess what colleges want you to say. They are not picky about what you say. They are interested in your ability to express yourself in writing. Whether readers agree with you is not the issue. In fact, it is often more interesting for the reader when there is some disagreement, but that is out of your control.

## *Standing Out in the Crowd*

Once again, take advantage of this opportunity to put on parade all the things that are the very essence of your individuality. Readers are interested in what makes you different. Remember, they are trying to assemble a class of interesting people who will collectively be able to contribute their individual talents and strengths to the college community. Don't fight it. Go with it. In your own way, tell them why you are interesting enough to be a member of that class.

## *Conditioning Your Mind*

Paul C. Zolbrod, the Frederick F. Seely Professor of English at Allegheny College in Pennsylvania, draws an interesting parallel between the preparation of good athletes and good students. Writing first in the Pittsburgh *Post-Gazette* and then in the February 12, 1992, issue of the *NCAA News,* he observes:

> Ironically, while their athletics teams benefit from well-conditioned, highly motivated players attracted to sports as kids, U.S. colleges and universities enroll underachieving young adults unprepared for the rigors of the classroom.

> As a college teacher in this post-literate, TV-saturated age, I wish more entering freshmen could construct sentences or handle equations the way college-bound athletes can tackle, jump or swing a bat.

> Society expects these young people to become statesmen, engineers, and problem solvers; yet many can't read a map, identify the subject of a sentence or calculate a square root. It is as if basketball players reported to their coaches unable to dribble while still expected to win games.

> What kind of society is it, I find myself wondering, where kids learn to apply themselves for hours in the gym or on the field but have not been taught to sit intently at a desk diagramming sen-

tences or adding fractions? Or for that matter, where fans may expect more of shortstops than parents expect of teachers—or teachers demand of students?

Believe it or not, good coaching can help. Just as college professors work with students to cultivate higher-order skills like syntheses and critical analysis, coaches engender complex plays and sophisticated game strategy.

And just as coaches know that athletes must first practice and master an effective stroke or a firm swing, teachers should expect youngsters to begin with simple skills, to accept criticism, to defer gratification, to discipline themselves as they learn. Whether in winning on the field or succeeding in class, the deepest fulfillment comes from performing well, which means mastering fundamentals first.

Once you begin making them, useful comparisons between sports and today's classroom readily occur. Because many freshmen have done so little writing by the time they come to college, they believe they need only sit at a computer the night before an essay is due and throw words on a screen.

But a seasoned athlete has learned that games aren't played that way. A good writer knows in advance precisely what he or she wants to say and knows how to say it, too—which means first laboring to develop an outline the way a team builds a game plan, or defining words and phrases one by one, the way a backfield runs a play over and over.

If we want our kids to learn as badly as young athletes want to wrestle or play tennis, we might experiment with methods coaches employ. We could instill in them the same intensity that a good team applies in a crucial game. We could point out to them that the rule of steady, patient practice prevails as readily in learning math as it does in passing the baton smoothly in a relay race.

As a college teacher formerly indifferent to sports, I gradually discovered that good athletes could discipline themselves to learn classroom fundamentals. They knew what it meant to try harder after getting beaten on a play, or to repeat a new move again and again. I simply reminded them how much alike study and practice are in mastering fundamentals.

Many of you are athletes who will relate very easily to what Professor Zolbrod says. Your ability to create a powerful paragraph will give you the same rush as sacking the quarterback, spiking a volleyball, acing your serve, earning a triple-double, or a host of other athletic accomplishments—maybe even more. You wouldn't be reading this book if you were not interested in improving your writing skills. To be good at something requires a great deal of practice, and we all know that practice makes perfect. Therein lies the lesson.

# The Essay as an Application Component

Writing in the winter 1992 issue of the *Journal of College Admission,* Cleve Latham, director of college guidance at the McCallie School in Tennessee, observed regarding the college application essay:

> "The most important writing we see in the college admission process, however, is from the student applicant. Or it should be. Could be. It should be the only thing needed to evaluate a candidate's academic promise. It could be a clue to the sort of instruction the candidate's school is offering. It should be a way for the student to write about what's on *his* mind, to tell the reader what he *wants* to be known about the life behind his academic persona."

College applications may vary in size and shape, but, for

the most part, the information that is being gleaned is the same. After all, colleges do have to know your name and address and other biographical information in order to proceed with you as a candidate. As you begin filling out your applications, you will find yourself sailing merrily along, completing all the boxes and blanks, until you hit the essay, and then, as they say, the plot really thickens, the rubber meets the road, it's crunch time. Now you have to think, and that takes time and energy and patience and imagination and resourcefulness—the very qualities colleges are looking for in applicants. Insecurity sets in, and you get that queasy feeling that you are heading into the Twilight Zone.

## Orderliness

One of the things the application does is to establish whether you are an orderly individual. Its overall appearance creates an impression in the mind of the reader, and, it should be added, a positive or negative bias. If, for example, you write or print illegibly and have a tendency to smudge your work or crumple it into an envelope too small for its size, the impression created is that you don't care, and the only reason you are going through with the exercise is because you have to. While this may be the truth, it is imprudent for you to openly admit it. It would be wiser for you to take care with your application.

Conversely, a very neat-appearing application creates a positive bias in the mind of the reader. A conscientious applicant is obviously taking this whole thing seriously. This applicant is trying hard to package himself or herself in the most attractive manner possible. Think about it. Wouldn't you much prefer to read a document submitted by someone who took care in its presentation?

The application form does allow space for your essay, but the space always seems to be inadequate. Accept this as a fact and use extra sheets of blank paper for your writing. It is perfectly acceptable for you to ignore the space devoted to the essay on the application form in favor of a separate document. Make certain that your name is on each page of your presentation. Admissions offices are swamped with paper during the height of the admissions season, and it is very easy for someone to inadvertently misplace a piece of unidentifiable paper.

Unless you have excellent penmanship, it is always wise to type your application; this includes the essay. Once again, if you place yourself in the position of the reader, you will agree that it would be much easier and quicker to read a typed manuscript than trying to decipher the gobbledegook with which some people are afflicted. Readers who are under the gun to wade through hundreds of essays in a relatively short space of time will not spend time on an illegible presentation.

*Originality*  As one of the components of the application, the essay stands out because it is really the only component that is devoted to originality. All the rest is known biographical information, and there is no guesswork or game-playing as to what details a college wants from you. Until you reach the essay, you are operating in very secure surroundings. You know for sure how old you are and on what street you live and in what town you live and how tall you are and how much you weigh. This is easy stuff, and you wish that were it. By the time you reach the end of the "easy stuff" on the application and come to the essay, panic begins to grip you. You are convinced that this must be a diabolical plot hatched by a collusive group of colleges to bring about your rejection. If the Justice Department can launch an investigation into alleged collusion on the part of some colleges in awarding financial aid, then there must be some high-profile governmental agency available to investigate why all colleges want to view your written work and why so many of them ask the same essay questions. You can wonder about that all you want, but, the fact of the matter is, you still must submit an essay to most, if not all, of the colleges to which you are applying.

What about applying to places like the University of Michigan or the University of Southern California? Do they require essays? And, if they do, are those essays actually read? Some applicants have strong reservations about the ability of admissions staffs at such large and popular institutions to find the time to read thousands of essays. Well, both institutions do require essays, and they are all read by someone. Cliff Sjogren, former long-time dean of admissions at Michigan and currently dean of admissions and financial aid at USC says about the essay, "Yes! Yes! Yes! We did read the essay at Michigan. Even though the university is a large public one, we did have a compression of quality kids from the top of their classes and the essay sometimes (not often) made the difference.

"And we read them at USC. We are more interested in the personal characteristics that are revealed in the essay than we are in the prose, although sloppy writing may be a 'negative.' Many applicants are from unsophisticated homes and schools, and to assign a standard factor for the essay to be applied to all applicants would be unfair and could result in improper decisions. I fear that some students are at an advantage in the admissions process (certainly not the education process) because they attended a senior English class that featured the college essay as a fall project, or they were financially able to hire a professional essay writer, a growing group of entrepreneurs.

"While the essay rarely influences a decision, I feel that it should be required. Sometimes clues emerge that explain an inconsistent academic record or a misunderstanding of the curricular choice (e.g. oceanography vs. marine engineering). The well-written essay will provide college advisors with some helpful understandings about the interests and the character of the student that might aid in the counseling process.

"Good essays will reveal interesting insights into the applicant's personality. Humor, if in good taste, and informality are acceptable. Dare to be different! Short essays (one page) are usually more desirable than long ones. Typing the essay is okay, but if a word processor is used, be sure to enter the proper variables. Several applicants to Michigan forgot to replace the name 'Cornell' as their 'first choice' college."

It is quite obvious that your essay will be read no matter the size of the institution to which you are applying. This should give you comfort for a couple of reasons: your effort will not be wasted and someone will be looking forward to reading what you have to say. Now your mindset becomes important. Actually, when you approach the essay with a positive attitude—that writing it is more a challenge than a chore—you will realize that here is your chance to strut your stuff. It is your only opportunity in completing your application to show some originality.

For many of you, this is unfamiliar territory, and, as such, it gives you an uncomfortable feeling that ranges anywhere from mild concern to downright fright. It may be consoling for you to realize that you are not the only one so afflicted. You have many peers across the land, at about the same time, who are also suffering. You should also know that the people who run the offices of admission are well aware of your concerns and nervousness and are more than willing to be sympathetic and understanding. The essay and the interview are, without doubt, the causes of most of the insecurity you will experience in the transition from secondary school to college. Do not worry; this insecurity is short-lived and, in retrospect, will make you wonder why you ever had a concern in the first place. All you need to do is be yourself, and things will work out just fine.

# How Much the Essay Counts

Secondary school seniors are often anxious to know the various weightings colleges give to all the components involved in the admissions process. They can then figure out where to devote their energy while, at the same time, relaxing their efforts when dealing with those components receiving less weight. This is a good example of the games students play when they engage in the admissions process. Students try to figure out what colleges want so they can comply. This is exactly the kind of gamesmanship colleges try very hard to avoid. Usually colleges consider all components to be equal. In fact, whether this is true is debatable and also unimportant in this context. You will, most likely, consider this an unacceptable answer.

Students often seem to want the whole broken down into segments, with specific weight assigned to each segment. College admissions does not work that way. Let's assume that readers use a rating scale of 10. Depending on the reader, a rating could be anywhere from 1 to 10. Members of the same admissions staff often disagree widely on the value of an essay. Some think that the essay gives the staff the best chance of getting to know a candidate and of learning what kind of writing habits a candidate has. It also underscores such characteristics as logic, humor, analysis, neatness, and care. This group of readers actually looks forward to the "reading phase" of the admissions year. For them, it is the time of year when they get the opportunity to discover the sensitivities, or lack thereof, in the applicant pool—sensitivities such as prejudice, love, hate, joy, anger, frustration—all the things that make us different and so interesting as individuals. Granted, all the reading represents the consumption of a great deal of time and energy, but it also serves as a tonic for many admissions people. It is important for you to realize that admissions readers are basically on your side in hoping that your written work will come out the way you want it to. If it does, they will be your "friend in court" and, if necessary, go to your defense when the final decisions are made.

This is one of the reasons it is so important for you to proofread your writing carefully prior to mailing it. If you fail to check spelling and grammar, you will create the impression that you don't care, that you are normally inattentive to detail, that you are less than enthusiastic about what you are doing, and, generally, that you have little pride in your work. When you consider what is at stake, these are hardly the impressions you want to create. More on this later.

A minority of readers is less enthusiastic about the "reading phase" of the admissions year. As a matter of fact, they are not fans of the essay requirement. They are skeptics. Every office staff has its share of skeptics. The primary doubt in the minds of these readers is who actually wrote the essay. We have all heard or read of the "essay mills," which, for a price, will provide an essay on any topic and package it to perfection for posting. There is no foolproof way to determine who the author is. However, do not give serious consideration to such an approach because experienced readers have a nose for sniffing out such chicanery. The good news about this group of readers is that they are a distinct minority who raise little or no objections to other staff members' taking the essay requirement more seriously.

Your best bet is to take the essay very seriously and assume that it will carry much weight in the final analysis.

Alfred T. Quirk, who has been the dean of admissions and financial aid at Dartmouth College in Hanover, New

Hampshire, for many years observes, "I am not sure that I can honestly say that I have seen that many essays over the years that are truly memorable, and perhaps that's my problem, and perhaps that's because of the way I approach folder reading. Primarily I look for consistency, and maybe that's why I'm not retentive enough. In other words, if the whole file smacks of mediocrity, I am not surprised when the essays don't move me, and it may be that when I am in that mode there are some real zingers that I am missing.

"My main concern in reading an essay is to determine if the student has really put some effort into it and is giving evidence of knowing what his or her teachers and counselor have said that he or she knows. I must say that sometimes I am put off when an English teacher writes about a student in glowing terms when there appears little evidence of ability to write in the essays. On the other hand, I have been favorably impressed to read an essay from a student who described a long and drawn-out year with a very demanding teacher, and then finding that the recommendation was from that teacher, and best of all finding that the two went together. So I guess my cryptic comment would be that if I find internal consistency in the essay, I am satisfied, and, like most of us, if the essay is too good, I get suspicious."

# What an Application Essay Is

One of the concerns you must have early on in the process of writing your college essay is to establish, in your own mind, just what an essay is. You know that it is something that you have to write. You know it must be long enough to look respectable. You have a pretty good idea that it should say something that represents your personality, abilities, and ideas. Otherwise, why would colleges want you to send them a writing sample? You can figure that whatever you submit will go under some kind of microscope with varying degrees of lens power. This realization should make you want to have a particularly good finished product. You also know that writing an essay is not how you prefer to spend your spare time, but it's time to go to college, and colleges all like essays.

So what is an essay?

***Defining an Essay***   As you know, the dictionary often gives more than one definition of the word you are seeking, thereby allowing you to choose the definition you think most appropriate. For our purposes, we will choose the following definition:

> "An essay is an analytic or interpretive literary composition usually dealing with its subject from a limited or personal point of view."

Those who read your written work will accept this definition and, most probably, attach some expectations to it—but more on that later.

Let's just take a moment to analyze this definition. An essay is a form of composition. It seems as though you have been writing compositions since time began. This is no big deal for you. Anybody with a basic knowledge of freshman English knows what a composition is. It has a subject that is clearly defined, developed, and played out to a logical conclusion. You are to choose the subject. This gives you a certain amount of freedom.

The subject with which you are to deal may come from a limited or personal point of view. If you are writing from the limited point of view, the implication is that a great deal of research is not required. The fact that you will have to do little or no research should please you, given the hectic schedule you are under as you wend your way toward graduation.

Although the subject may be dealt with more objectively than when you take a personal point of view, days of painstaking fact-finding are not necessary. However, if you choose this approach, you must be careful that any numbers, percentages, quotes, or other factual information that you use in support of your point of view are accurate and that your sources are clearly identified. The same applies to any personal opinions you may express. Extensive research is not really necessary, but sources for supporting statements should be identified. Nothing detracts more from credibility than general and sweeping statements that just beg for some kind of factual support.

What is called for is that you take a stand on a topic of your choice. It would be a good idea for you to toss around several different topics in your mind as you go about your daily business to determine whether you really do have strong feelings before you plunge into the actual writing.

*Expressing Yourself*   You should view this exercise as a wonderful opportunity for self-expression. Someone is actually giving you the chance to say what you think and allowing you to call upon whatever resources you can muster to defend the position you may take. Obviously, there is a good deal of personal opinion involved, and readers are going to be very interested in what you have to say. So you had better have something to say. Readers are also going to be interested in how you support your opinions and will be looking forward to how you develop your thoughts. Personal opinions should be accentuated and clearly defined and presented so that readers will have no trouble following the "bouncing ball."

It is a good idea to take some preliminary time to read just a few of the works of the great literary essayists such as Jonathan Swift, Ralph Waldo Emerson, and Sir Francis Bacon. This kind of research will tend to give you a better perspective on what you are about. In his essay "Hints Towards an Essay on Conversation," Swift wrote, "I was prompted to write my thoughts upon this subject by mere indignation, to reflect that so useful and innocent a pleasure, so fitted for every period and condition of life, and so much in all men's power, should be so much neglected and abused." You see, strong feelings—in this case indignation—caused him to take pen in hand to get it off his chest.

Bacon once wrote an essay called "Of Marriage and Single Life." He wrote, "He that hath wife and children hath given hostages to fortune; for they are impediments to great enterprises, either of virtue or mischief. Certainly the best works, and of greatest merit for the public, have proceeded from the unmarried or childless men; which both in affection and means have married and endowed the public." From our perspective in the 1990s, Bacon's words seem to be filled with controversy and sexism.

Ralph Waldo Emerson always packs a wallop with his words. Here are three sentences from his essay "Self Reliance": "Trust thyself: every heart vibrates to that iron string," "Whoso would be a man, must be a nonconformist," and "A foolish consistency is the hobgoblin of little minds, adored by little statesmen and philosophers and divines." It is not expected, but perfectly permissable, that you be as provocative. However, reading a few of the essays that these three wrote will give you a better understanding of the objective.

Alan B. Crocker, college advisor at Saint Mark's School in Southborough, Massachusetts, writes, "The essay is the one time in the application process that the student can speak on their own behalf. It is important to write well but equally important is to be able to tell the admissions officer something more about yourself. This essay is an example of your best work; take time to write well and say something that will lead to a better understanding of who you really are. Remember, your teachers have written a recommendation on your behalf, your guidance counselor has written on your behalf. This is your opportunity to help yourself; make the most of it."

## *Keeping Your Essay Brief*

You will notice that nothing has been mentioned about how long your essay should be. Colleges never say much about this, so you may assume that you control length. You should remember, however, that readers have many essays to read and that they agree that brevity is a virtue. Ronald D. Potier, director of admissions at Elizabethtown College in Pennsylvania, suggests the following, "Students writing a college essay should assume that it will be the last one reviewed by the admissions officer that day or evening. They should understand that fatigue and boredom have probably set in and that the reader might be at their lowest attention span level. If the writer directs their message with crispness and originality, they will recapture the reader's attention. Naturally all essays will not be the 'last one read'; however, if the writer makes that assumption, then their attempts should have that little extra zip and spark that we all look for."

You will find as you grow older that the ability to summarize becomes a prized objective. People do not want to hear the long version of anything. They are much more interested in, and receptive to, the short version. If you can get your point across in one paragraph, why take four paragraphs? If you have a tendency to ramble on in your speech or writing, you run the risk of losing the interest of whomever you are addressing. You are living in a sound-byte era, so you should be aware that brevity is a virtue.

## *Elements of an Essay*

An essay has four basic elements:

1. An idea,

2. An outline,

3. A vocabulary,

4. Delivery.

The dictionary has several definitions for the word "idea." The one most suitable to this context is, ". . . a formulated thought or opinion." The idea is the element from which the rest of the elements draw sustenance. It is the subject of the discourse. It is the core of your thinking and, hence, of your essay. If you have strong feelings about your idea, it will show in terms of expression, enthusiasm, and conviction. Ideas are all around you. They generally come from personal experiences related to school, a job, a hobby, a relationship, a political or social issue, etc. Once you select an idea think about what you're going to say. If you cannot carry the idea through to a logical conclusion, go back to the drawing board. Conversely, if you like the way your thinking evolves go full speed ahead.

Your outline will be your "game plan." We'll discuss the outline in greater detail on pages 29–31, but, for now, remember that the creation of an outline will provide you with firm ground upon which to stand as you proceed with your writing. It will prevent you from wandering with your thinking. It will keep you on track. An outline to a writer is similar to a blueprint for a builder, a pattern for a seamstress, or a game plan for a coach.

The third element is vocabulary. The greater your vocabulary, the greater the ease with which you will write your essay. Choose words that befit a teenage author. Choose words that you use in everyday conversation. If you have a limited vocabulary, it would be a very good idea for you to decide right now to create a program of self-study aimed at expanding it. You are judged by the words you use. If you don't know many words, you will find doors closing to you as you pass through life. Familiarize yourself with action verbs and descriptive adjectives which can add interest to your writing. Improving your vocabulary will cost you very little in the way of time and money, and the results will be incredibly satisfying.

And, finally, we come to the delivery. This is the actual writing. You want to make sure that you get your points across and that there is a sensible flow from one point to the next. You begin with your introduction and you close with your ending. In between, you make your points. The introduction tells what your subject is and why you are presenting it. The mid-section develops and supports your points. The conclusion summarizes what you have written.

The fact that you are in complete control of the whole exercise is a real plus. You decide what you are going to write about. You decide how long your essay is going to be. You decide whether it will be funny or sad, long or short, subjective or objective, poignant or playful, critical or complimentary. An overwhelming majority of admissions officers believe that the essay represents a fine opportunity for you to put your uniqueness on parade. If you take the same viewpoint, you will place yourself in a wonderfully positive state of mind. And that will be half the battle for you.

## The Range of Topics

Since most of the application forms with which you will be dealing offer a choice of three or four topics, choosing a topic will not be a major problem. However, what happens when you are not comfortable with any of the suggested topics? The question is really, "Do I have the liberty of picking a topic on my own? Is it permissable to ignore the choices that are offered on the application form?" The answer is that you will most probably be allowed to be original.

If you request application forms from 100 different colleges, you will find very little variance in terms of the suggested topics. After all, there are only so many interesting suggestions. One of the strategies in assigning a topic is to determine how well you deal with a subject not of your choice. It is much more testing to deal with a topic not of your choice. Here are some essay questions gleaned from a random selection of college application forms.

- Describe what you feel has been a significant event in your life.

- Please review the following list of important admissions criteria. Your academic record, which includes both the quality of your performance and the difficulty of your program, is most important to us in our review of candidates and has, therefore, been marked #1. After reading through the alphabetical list below, rank the remaining criteria in the order of their importance to you. List only your top three choices (2-3-4). In an essay in the space below, briefly explain your reasons for selecting this rank order.

  Academic Record (grades, quality of program)
  Achievement Test Scores (CEEB)
  Class Rank
  Community Service
  Creative Expression
  Extracurricular Involvement
  Leadership Record

Personal Experiences
Potential to Contribute to the College Community
SAT/ACT Scores

- Evaluate a significant experience or achievement that has special meaning for you.

- Discuss some issue of personal, local, or national concern and its importance to you.

- Describe the person whom you would choose as your hero or heroine. Please explain how this person exemplifies the ideals which you value.

- Write on one of the following:

  1. "The most beautiful thing we can experience is the mysterious. It is the source of all true art and science.
     Albert Einstein, "What I Believe"

  2. "It was books that taught me that the things that tormented me most were the very things that connected me with all people who were alive, or who had ever been alive.
     James Baldwin

  3. "Lying is done with words and also with silence."
     Adrienne Rich

  4. "The problem with the future is that it keeps turning into the present."
     Hobbes, "Calvin and Hobbes"

  5. "No man can know where he is going unless he knows exactly where he has been and exactly how he arrived at his present place."
     Maya Angelou

  6. "People have to believe in their capacity to act and bring about a good result. Leaders must help them keep that enlivening belief."
     John W. Gardner, "The Tasks of Leadership"

If you absolutely dislike the choices offered, it is always possible to communicate with the admissions office in question and request permission to write on a topic of your choosing. This is best done in writing because you will then have a record of such approval—and then make sure to save the response. If you prefer to make such a request by phone, you should make certain that you record the name and title of the person with whom you speak and then append your essay with a brief note explaining the situation and mentioning the name and title of the person granting the permission. It is worth noting that the person granting the permission should be a bonafide member of the admissions staff rather than a member of the support staff or a part-time interviewer. Taking the liberty of making such a request may make a positive impression, because too many applicants are intimidated into thinking that they must pick one of the choices offered under penalty of rejection.

It may be that your request for a topic of your choosing will be denied, but the chances are slim. Be sure you have a topic and reasons for backing up your choice before you take pen in hand or pick up the phone to make your request. Given a legitimate rationale, most colleges, if not all, will grant your request and be impressed with your independence and desire to be original. If, in the unlikely event your request is denied, then you bite the bullet and do the best you can. Angels can do no more. It all goes under the heading, "Nothing ventured, nothing gained." Pay attention to the old English proverb: "Many things are lost for want of asking."

# Choosing Your Topic

You should know that such a thing as a *common application* exists. It is a form subscribed to by approximately 115 colleges and universities across the country. The purpose of this form is to facilitate the process of applying to college. It must be completed only once, with photocopies of the "Application for Undergraduate Admission," "School Report," and "Teacher Evaluation" sent to any number of participating colleges. The procedure simplifies the college application process by saving time and eliminating unnecessary duplication of effort.

The 1991–92 common application form has a section entitled "Personal Statement." The section reads as follows:

> "This personal statement helps us become acquainted with you in ways different from courses, grades, test scores, and other objective data. It enables you to demonstrate your ability

to organize thoughts and express yourself. Please write an essay about one of the topics listed below. You may attach extra pages (same size, please) if your essay exceeds the limits of this page.

1. Evaluate a significant experience or achievement that has special meaning to you.

2. Discuss some issue of personal, local, or national concern and its importance to you.

3. Indicate a person who has had a significant influence on you, and describe that influence."

It is fairly safe to assume that these topics represent the collective thinking of member colleges and universities. Many will appear on the application forms of nonmember colleges because they are regarded to be good topics. You may want to roll these around in your head for a while because of their universality.

## Thinking About Your Options

If, after reviewing all the possible topics presented on the application forms with which you are working, you are not comfortable with any of your options, then it will be necessary to pick your own—to be original. Often, this is the most difficult part of the whole exercise. Many students have great difficulty selecting their own topic. Many of you will select a subject without giving it a great deal of thought and begin your writing only to find out that, as you progress, things are not playing out as you had hoped. A combination of factors comes into play, preventing the essay from developing as fully as it should.

You find that you did not take enough time to really mull over the subject—to let it roll around in your head long enough for you to carry the thought through to a logical conclusion. Before you start to write it is always a good idea to test your thinking with some of your family or friends. Run your topic by them. Ask them for their opinions and reactions to certain elements of the subject you intend to present. Such conversational exchanges will help you think your way through your subject and also present some new perspectives for you to consider. You will find that two heads are, indeed, better than one. You will also discover whether you have established an adequate comfort level with your subject. If not, you will rather quickly realize that the reactions you encounter from family and friends will become more of a hindrance than a help, and you will find yourself becoming more argumentative and less conversational as you seek reactions. If this is the result of your conversations, you may need to return to the "drawing board" in search of another topic.

We have already discussed the value of your having strong feelings about your chosen topic in order to make a more forceful presentation. Whether you are taking a pro or con position makes little difference as long as you show conviction in your writing. Remember that readers are faced with many essays to review. The forceful essays tend to stand out and to be remembered. If you take enough time with your approach, giving adequate thought to how your subject plays out to a logical conclusion, you will most probably be comfortable with your selection. You will also be able to take a position that will be clearly understood by the readers.

## Preparing Yourself

One of the advantages that you enjoy is that you control the timetable for the application process. At least once you decide that you are going to college and recognize and honor the various application deadlines, you are in control. Your college counselor has probably mentioned the essay sometime in your junior year, or your brother or sister or friend has mentioned to you that an essay will most likely be required when you fill out your college application. In other words, you will have, or have had, ample time to prepare yourself. And so you are in control. If you choose to procrastinate, you will be placing yourself under unnecessary pressure that may well adversely impact your ability to produce an essay representative of your talent and potential.

The more insecure you are about your writing abilities, the more prudent it would be for you to think about starting your essay toward the end of your junior year in secondary school or, certainly, during the summer prior to the start of your senior year. Such a timetable would allow plenty of time for trial and error with various subjects. It would allow you to "fool around" with topics that you extract from application forms you have requested or learned about from friends who have been through the exercise.

On the other hand, if you have great confidence in your writing abilities, you can delay to later in the fall of your senior year. However, you should be careful to allow yourself enough time to avoid the necessity of eleventh-hour heroics in order to meet deadlines. Remember, your senior year is going to be a very busy time for you and, at least until the end of the fall semester, quite demanding academically. Typically, social obligations will also increase when you start your final year.

In the fall term, you will also be facing the SAT or ACT and, perhaps, a few achievement tests. Some of you will be trying to schedule personal interviews or, at least, attempting to visit one or more campuses. You can readily see that you will be much more comfortable if you don't have the essay hanging over your head like the proverbial sword of Damocles. Do yourself a very big favor and get an early start.

If you stop and think about it, there are possible topics all around you: the homeless, environmental issues, divorce, abortion, unemployment, the greenhouse effect, the right to die, euthanasia, the peace dividend, feminism, racism, antisemitism, family relationships, peer relationships, boy/girl problems and so on. If possible, try to avoid topics that are a bit superficial such as "What Football Means to Me" or "My Summer Travels," unless you honestly feel that the experience has significantly altered your outlook on life. If so, make every effort to write poignantly and forcefully so that you will make a convert of the reader.

*A Sample Essay*

Here is an example of an original essay, the topic chosen by the writer, presented with feeling and, obviously, the product of tangible experience.

I finally have been taken out of the intensive care in the hospital and my name has been removed from the critical list, but I am still awaiting a complete recovery from a disease that all American Chinese have and that a few, like I, dread. This disease lies dormant in most American Chinese, but becomes malignant in the other unfortunate few. The symptoms of this disease are bipartitely divided, the first group of symptoms belonging to the majority of Chinese not malignantly affected by this disease. Their symptoms bring contentment, joy, and the assurance of a bright future. The second group belongs to those who are malignantly affected. Their symptoms bring anxiety, frustration, and deep pain. What is this bizarre malady that can bring either so much happiness or so much anguish? It is the Chinese Syndrome, a disease that only afflicts families with children.

It is not too hard to recognize the majority. They are the ABC's (American Born Chinese) with the 4.0 grade point averages and enough medals from piano competitions to recast the Statue of Liberty in gold. They are the ones who destroy all hopes of receiving a much needed curve on the AP Calculus II test. The minority is also quite easy to recognize. They are the ones who like seeing how many words they can assemble from their grades. They, however, often find themselves unable to form a coherent word because they lack a vowel. The majority also have a problem forming words. No matter how hard they try, they always end up sounding like Fonz on "Happy Days."

Where do the roots of this horrible disease lie? They lie, of course, within the parents. All parents, whether they are from the majority or the minority, have one tragic flaw: they are constantly in search of the elusive commodity called pride. It is a pride that lies in the parent's child who graduated from AP High as valedictorian or, with some reluctance of the parents, salutatorian. Many parents, in fact, perverse the function of dinner parties by creating family feuds in the living room of the hostess. Parents launch ICBM's (InCredibly Bombastic Material) of what stupendous grades and awards their children have recently acquired. Other families retaliate with barrages of how late their son stays up at night doing his homework or practicing piano. Even the hostess takes a good swing to the guests by blinding them with her daughter's violin competition awards as they walk through the door. But, what happens to the minorities' parents? They quietly slump down in their chairs, wishing that they were some miniscule blob in the next room.

These parents, however, get their revenge for this shocking embarrassment by dashing home and taking the culprit who must have mistakenly been born as their child and assailing him with the dreaded "look-at-Doug-who-got-a-690-verbal-and-a-780-math-and-won-the-state-competition-in-piano-and-got-into-Harvard" lecture. Even as the shell-shocked child limps away, he can still hear his parents ranting and raving in the kitchen below, asking why did they not get a child like Doug?

The strain and stress of these battered children is enormous. They cannot help but feel pain, frustration, and uselessness when they see that their achievements do not match up to their friends. I was once one of those orphans left out in the cold until I found the only possible cure for this disease. I found myself.

I finally was able to see my own special talents that define who I really am. With this discovery, I also found my self-worth and the ability to believe in myself. I no longer mope about the house, wondering why I was not blessed with the ability that many other Chinese have. Now, I realize that the talents I do have are special and unique in me.

Through my experience with this disease, a sense of maturity and self-realization has evolved. I am grateful for the efforts of my parents who are trying valiantly to prepare me for the future by making me the best that I can ever be. Often, we, the minority, feel that our parents' attitude toward the whole matter of being Chinese belongs in another century and world, but we must recognize our parents' concern for our future. Frequently, we are too short-sighted to see this. It is true that our parents are looking for pride, but everyone needs something to be proud about and there is nothing better than a parent being proud of his or her child.

Alas, this disease, the Chinese Syndrome, will never fade away. It will always be there to torment those few unfortunate Chinese who have not yet found themselves. Until they do so, they are lost in a world of sermons that last late into the night. We often find ourselves saying like Othello: "Farewell tranquil mind, farewell content." I still find myself studying hard in order to stay up with the pack that we Chinese make up. Within that pack is a gamut of raw talent and energy. It does not matter that I may not be like the majority of Chinese children. I am proud to be Chinese."

Understand that this is an example of an original topic that represents the strong convictions of the writer. As a piece of writing it has its shortcomings, and you can probably improve it through your changes and corrections. Fool around with it and see what you can do to improve it.

Susan Biemeret explains, "Finding the appropriate topic can be difficult. Often, students search for a particularly climactic moment to describe in the personal essay. Students agonize over the fact that they have never had a 'significant experience' about which to write an essay. Nothing could be further from the truth—each high school senior applying to college is the sum of myriad significant experiences which have formed and shaped his/her personality, value system, and thought process.

"Instead of focusing on some watershed in your life (very few adults have had such experiences), students should look inside themselves for the topic of an essay. Think about your relationship with your family, childhood events which have an impact on you today; academic experiences which shaped the way you think; people who have had a lasting effect upon your personality or value systems; or a personal cause, interest, or hobby that you want to share with others. When examined from this viewpoint, your life can become a series of significant experiences about which to write."

# Getting Psyched

A very wise person once observed, "You are what you think you are!" There is a strong message contained in this observation, and much of it has to do with confidence and self-esteem. If you are an exceptional athlete, it is probably because you have been blessed with a gift in the form of size or speed or coordination or all three. In fact, exceptional people, whether they be athletes or musicians or artists or writers, have been given a gift that most of us do not have. However, many of us are good, but not exceptional, at doing various things. We rely on practice and more practice until we are able to master our objective. As we become more proficient, we become more confident, and we feel better about ourselves and our performance.

Just think, if you put as much time into practicing your writing as you do with your sport or with your avocational interest, you might well surprise yourself as to your proficiency with the pen. If, as you face the application procedure, you think that having to write an essay is one of life's major crises, then it probably will be. You obviously lack confidence in your writing ability. Is this the case with you? Or do you look at the essay requirement as a challenge, an opportunity for you to respond to a suggested topic, or to pick your own and express your very personal thoughts?

Somehow you must get psyched for this exercise. There is no doubt—believe this, it is the truth—that everyone is pulling for you to do a good job with the essay. Everyone includes you, your parents, your boyfriend or girlfriend, your teachers, your guidance counselor, members of the various admissions staffs, your coaches, your grandparents—just about anyone with whom you share a relationship. So, for starters, you have many people on your side, people you do not want to disappoint.

### *Avoiding Procrastination*

We have already discussed how procrastination can be the real culprit in this exercise. You need to be aware that this may be a major pitfall for you. Right now, stop putting off your essay. Pull your chair up to your desk or the kitchen table or wherever you do such work and begin with an outline that will eventually grow into a first class essay.

The outline is critical to your thinking because it will supply the necessary discipline to keep you on target. It will become the base from which you operate. It will be the high ground on which you will stand, thereby preventing an occasional step into the quicksand of disjointed and irrelevant thinking. It will help you to crystallize your thinking. It may be the most important and difficult part of the whole exercise. Once your thoughts are set in the outline, you are well on your way to creating that first-class essay.

### *How to Make an Outline*

Let's assume that you want to write about the death of your father after a long battle with cancer. You want to make certain that you mention the affect it had on you and the rest of your family. From your perspective, you also want to expound on the mystery of death and why your father was taken from you. You may think about creating the following outline:

1. Death in the family (brief description of family)

   A. Father (give some personal characteristics and the role he played)

   B. Reactions (simple declarative statement of grief)
   a. Family (how each has been affected)
   b. You (how you have been affected)

   C. Support (where does your support come from?)

2. Coping (how the family is adjusting)

   A. Mourning (mention protocol)
   a. obituary
   b. funeral arrangements
   c. calling hours
   d. funeral (how these all help keep you busy)

   B. Recovery (how you are returning to normal)

3. Lessons learned

   A. The finality of it all
   a. the inevitable void
   b. the power of prayer

   B. Time is a healer
   a. getting through the immediate stress
   b. getting on with your life

   C. Be more demonstrable (you never really said how you feel)

4. Death and dying

   A. The indignity of it all

   B. Why my family?

   C. Memories become a positive force

Actually, the outline is little more than a control system that prevents wandering. Once you decide what you want to write about, you should decide what thoughts will support your premise. Working from the general to the specific, you place these thoughts in the form of an outline. In turn, the outline will keep you on track until you have fully expressed yourself.

You may write as much or as little as you wish under each heading. The amount of verbiage will be governed by your individual feelings.

The more you try to avoid getting started with your writing, the more pressure you will create for yourself.

Your educational experience, probably at least sixteen years to date, should have given you the tools with which to work. All the time you spent in those elementary school spelling bees and diagramming sentences in junior high or lower school and with secondary school book reports, research papers, and general writing assignments should have prepared you for any writing you are required to do now.

## Building Self-Esteem

If you are reading this book, it is safe to assume that you have successfully completed the tenth grade and, most probably, the eleventh grade and are heading into the final year of secondary school. This is quite an accomplishment, something about which you can be proud. Only you can determine whether your level of achievement thus far is a source of pride for you. If it is, you must feel pretty good about yourself. Your self-esteem is high, and that is good. You have developed into an interesting person.

College admissions people make a career out of meeting and cultivating interesting people. Their primary task each year is to select, enroll, and introduce an interesting group of young people to their respective college communities. One of the best ways for them to establish whether a person is interesting is through his or her essay.

It seems simple enough. We have an interesting person and we have a group looking for interesting people. One of the instruments that is used to bring them together is called the college application essay. Sue Biemeret, college consultant at Adlai Stevenson High School, remarks:

> "Why is the essay so important? The purpose of an essay is to allow the applicant to rise above all the statistical data on the application (the grade point average, test scores, rank) to reflect the subjective side of the application process. Students have a chance to let the college see the person behind all that raw data.

> "If students approach the writing as a positive experience, the results will be well worth it. It's even possible to enjoy the writing of the essay, as students will find the entire process to be thought-provoking, insightful, and personally revealing."

There you have it. You have all the tools necessary to do a good job. You have pride in your work. You are an interesting person. Your educational experience has prepared you for this moment. What you have to say is going to be important. What are you waiting for? Show admissions people, and yourself, what you can do when you set your mind to it.

John Yatchisin, assistant dean of admissions and financial aid at Colby-Sawyer College, New London, New Hampshire, says:

> "Having worked in both large and small institutions of higher learning, I consider the college admissions essay to be crucial to my understanding of a candidate and what he or she has to offer. Most of what we review in a student's admissions application is quantitative, and in the absence of an interview the college admissions essay is the best means of getting a qualitative grasp of the person involved. Remember, colleges do care about you as a person, and how you will fit into their community. Use your essay to tell a college who you are, and what is important to you. Show off your creativity and your passion—who knows, it might make the difference between acceptance and denial at your 'first choice' school."

*Be Yourself*    Did you ever try to counsel an introvert to become an extrovert or vice versa? Can a leopard really change its spots? In most instances, we are what we are, and we should do the best we can with whatever that may be. Most of you reading this book are either sixteen or seventeen years of age. Most of you have not yet fully developed your writing capabilities. As your education and experience expand, so will your ability to express yourself. People who will read your essay are very much aware of this type of evolution and will be sympathetic to and understanding of your status. The most important thing for you to remember in this regard is that you be yourself.

The real you should write as though you were speaking to a friend in the quiet of your living room or kitchen. If, in your proofreading, your writing sounds as though it came from someone other than yourself, it will most likely impress the reader the same way. For example, if you do not use what some of us would call sophisticated words when you speak to your friends, then you should avoid using them in your writing. Being yourself will allow you to be much more comfortable, and that comfort will manifest itself in your writing.

The general vocabulary of an educated person, the result of education and experience and reading and paying attention to all three, is usually quite different from the vocabulary of a sixteen- or seventeen-year-old. The words are more sophisticated, and they are used in the proper context. Experience in using words over time allows an adult to be able to invoke the right word at the right time. If you are a reader, then you probably possess an unusually strong vocabulary for your age, and you have the knack of choosing the right word at the right time. Now is the time to put your ability on parade. But make sure your choice of words fits the context.

On the other hand, if you have studiously avoided reading anything that you were not absolutely required to read and your vocabulary is limited, it would be prudent for you to stick to using the words you know and love and use every day. In short, don't try to be an educational sophisticate by using those "big words" that are not a part of your everyday lexicon. Simple sentences peppered with action verbs and descriptive adjectives befitting a teenager are not only acceptable but also preferred.

However, there are some words and phrases that should be stricken from your vocabulary as soon as you read this. They are: *like, I mean, you know, right?*. None of them adds class, intelligence, substance, or panache to your expression. On the contrary, they probably do suggest insecurity, laziness, and like, you know, I mean, intellectual immaturity. Right now and always banish them from your personal lexicon—right?

Lengthy, run-on sentences are unacceptable. They give the impression that your mind is just running on with no direction or boundaries to your thinking. When you speak or write, you do so to express a feeling or point of view. Be certain that you are clear in your expression to your reader. Don't leave the reader to guess what you are trying to say. Simple sentences carry great power in terms of clarity and directness. Use simple sentences whenever possible.

Once in a while, it is not only a good idea but also helpful to use a famous quotation or two to sprinkle a little of what the French call *savoir faire* into your writing. The sayings of famous people can help you make a point, because, in most instances, they have stated something better than you ever could and probably more succinctly.

However, if you inject too many quotations, they will begin to take over your writing, and this is hardly your objective. Everything in moderation.

In this day of technological advances, you can enjoy a growing number of hardware and software aids. If you are fortunate enough to have the use of word processing equipment, you understand the point. It is a good idea to take advantage of these aids. If you are a poor speller, there is software to prevent you from making your weakness public knowledge. If you are a poor grammarian, there is software that will make you look like you wrote the book on diagramming sentences. Your friendly, neighborhood computer store will be more than happy to help you find some of these software saviors.

There are always the thesaurus and the dictionary. You should certainly familiarize yourself with the section in the back of your dictionary entitled "Handbook of Style." Strunk and White's *The Elements of Style* is also a useful, time-proven aid for writers at all levels of ability.

Phyllis Steinbrecher, a well-known independent educational consultant from Westport, Connecticut, makes the following observations,

> "The college essay offers each candidate a special opportunity to talk directly to an admissions committee. It is not what anyone has to say about you—it is what you have to say about yourself! Your personal statement should be written, re-written, and written again until it truly reflects you as a person. Through your essay, colleges can learn what you feel most enthusiastic about, what your talents, and unique experiences have been, how you demonstrate leadership and the personal qualities you feel are most important for others to understand about you. Try to discuss what sets you apart from anyone else.

> "If a college asks a specific question, answer what they ask and don't stray from the topic. As you write, keep in mind that brevity and clarity are virtues, that depth is more important than breadth, that you should use specific examples from your own life and avoid generalizations, that it is very important to be honest and that, most of all, it is important to be yourself.

> "Start drafting your essay the summer before your senior year. You will need the time. Write a

draft and put it away for twenty-four hours. Read it. Is it focused? Boring? Interesting? Would you respond favorably to the person it describes? Rewrite it. Then, repeat those two steps until you really like what you've written and are satisfied that it tells your story well. Have someone you respect read it and comment candidly about it. Check carefully for grammar and spelling errors. Read the essay aloud to see how it reads. Type or write your essay carefully. Send it on its way."

# The Ultimate Crutch: The Five-Paragraph Theme

Those of you who take pleasure in writing exercises may choose to skip this chapter, because it really is not directed at you. It is included for those who are having trouble coming to grips with their college application requirement. Many of you have already been exposed to the five-paragraph theme somewhere along the line. Some of you may not remember such exposure because you were more interested in something else at the time. It was most likely introduced back in middle or lower school when a fairly serious approach to writing should have taken place.

There was a time when colleges gave English placement examinations to first-year students, and tested their writing abilities. Those who did not measure up were required to take an English composition course which included such basic exercises as diagramming sentences and writing expository and imaginative essays and five-paragraph themes. Many students still benefit from the things they learned in their refresher course. Most colleges have long since abandoned this testing on the assumption that these basics should have been taught in the lower grades—all of which once again proves the old adage that you can never assume anything.

The five-paragraph theme really does serve well as a crutch. It is easy to understand and fairly easy to carry out. It does not require brilliance in terms of writing ability nor does it demand an unusual amount of imagination. It forces you to abide by certain constraints that prevent a variety of writing sins. It will also give you some good training at thinking about what you are going to say before you say it. And yet it will confine your writing to the subject at hand, because five paragraphs is not an overload to your thinking mechanism. You can easily handle your thoughts from start to finish.

Whether your topic is chosen from those offered or is an original makes no difference. You will find the five-paragraph approach is nondiscriminatory; it will fit any topic. Let's take a look.

You use the first paragraph to introduce your topic. We have already talked about how brevity is considered a virtue. Please remember this. None of these paragraphs need to be long and rambling. After you use a sentence or two to introduce the topic, you should follow with another sentence to introduce the three main points you are going to make in support of your position on the main topic.

These three points can be included in one sentence and presented in a series separated by commas or semicolons; check your grammar book if you are unsure of how to use these punctuation marks correctly. It would be nice if you could close your paragraph with a strong transitional sentence to comfortably and subtly transfer the thinking of the reader to your next paragraph.

Actually, it would be prudent for you always to think about strong transitional sentences whenever you are creating building blocks of thought. You will be amazed at how well transitions allow your audience to follow your line of thinking and how easy it is for you to get your point across. Make a mental note of this. It applies to any type of communication.

As you begin paragraph two, check the preceding paragraph where you listed your three main points. Make sure you select the first point and include it in your first sentence. Then write a few sentences in support of your point. After you finish the paragraph, read it over carefully. Does it make the point you want made? If so, does it do it forcefully enough? Does it make sense to you? Does it read well?

Does the last sentence of paragraph two satisfactorily transfer your thinking to the first sentence of paragraph three? If it just doesn't read right to you, chances are that it will not read right to others. Give it some more thought and rework it. Or proceed with the rest of the essay and then go back and make your review and assessment within the totality of your writing.

Paragraph three is going to deal with point number two and paragraph four is going to deal with point number three. You use the same approach each time. You critique it the same way each time.

Now, you come to paragraph five. This is where you exit. This is the paragraph you use to say goodbye. You may want to think about a brief summary statement to underscore and emphasize what you have already written. Writing clearly is similar to being in a foreign country and not having great success in being understood by the locals. You find yourself having to tell them what you are going to tell them, then telling them, then telling them what you told them. The point is to make certain that no person will have any difficulty understanding what your message is. And so you read it as many times as necessary until you are satisfied that you have accomplished your objective. Then you have a couple of other people read it just to make sure they can recognize your message.

When you take some time to think about it, you can readily see how effective the five-paragraph theme can be. The rationale behind it is sound. It forces you to organize your thoughts, to present them clearly and simply, to get in and out cleanly with your subject matter, to be concise and succinct, and to leave no doubt about what the message is. This approach provides excellent training for your thought process, whether it is manifested in your writing or in your speech. You may just want to incorporate the rationale of this approach as standard operating procedure.

# Proofreading Your Essay

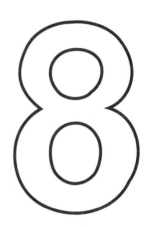

By the time you reach this stage of writing your college application essay, you should have a great sense of accomplishment. You have passed through the most difficult part of the whole exercise. There really is light at the end of the tunnel—and you can see it. There is only one thing left to do, and that is to proofread your work. It may be your most important responsibility. Take it very seriously.

The whole idea of proofreading is to make sure that the finished product is free of errors and says what you want to say in a convincing manner. People who work in college admissions are constantly frustrated by the flagrant disregard for proofreading shown by applicants. It is difficult to understand why applicants fail to realize the importance of checking their work.

In most cases, essays are not written in one sitting. Generally speaking, it may take two or three drafts before it sets up the way you want it. When you realize that those who read the essay are trying to find out what makes you tick, it suggests that you may want to give it your best effort. Certainly a good job of proofreading is part of the effort.

Make certain that you check your spelling and your punctuation. Know what adverbs are and how to use them correctly. Just in case their definition has slipped your mind Barron's *A Pocket Guide to Correct English* tells us that "an adverb usually modifies a verb telling how, where, when or why an action is done. It can also modify an adjective or another adverb. Except for very common ones, adverbs usually end in -ly." The American public has a distinct tendency to butcher adverbs. How often do you hear phrases such as, "He done good," or "It was real good," or "She felt bad about it"?

Have you used any double comparatives (more sweeter)? Have you used any double negatives (It doesn't make no difference to me.)? Have you mixed tenses (I had a milkshake that tastes very good.)? And always remember that you never end a sentence with a preposition (e.g., to, for, on, with—check your grammar book for other commonly used prepositions).

After you make your so-called technical check—grammar/spelling/punctuation—then read your essay over a couple of times to catch the flow. Does it deliver the message you intended? Do your thoughts lead from one to another smoothly? Have you adequately supported the points you are trying to make? Is your writing clear and concise? Are there any unanswered questions? If you are unhappy with the general tone, then you should rework the areas in question.

By all means, have someone else read your finished essay. Find someone whose writing ability you respect. This may produce comments that you really do not want to hear. But you should now be mature enough to cope with constructive criticism. Understand that it may mean that you will have to return to the drawing board for a rewrite. But if it is a desirable revision, one that will enhance your effort, then you have no alternative but to do it before you submit your work. A second and, possibly, a third opinion are always a good idea. Most offices that operate successfully in the marketplace will require two or three readings of any written communication prior to its distribution.

Until you feel very good about what you have written, your task has not been accomplished. Stay with it, because you do have the potential to achieve that feeling just like others who are also bright, confident, mature, sensitive, humorous, articulate, glib, and concise.

# A Potpourri of Essays

You are now aware that you may have the choice between writing on an assigned subject or a subject of your choosing. Even though you may be faced with an assigned subject, you will most likely have a choice of three or four topics. In all cases, you may wish to submit an optional essay as additional evidence of your writing ability or to make a point about a subject close to your heart.

Generally speaking, the optional essay will be of greatest interest to the better writers. Applicants who go into this essay requirement with their heels dug in will most likely want to say "thanks but no thanks," and that is perfectly acceptable. There is no penalty exacted on those who do not choose to write an optional essay.

On the other hand, it may present an advantage for some. Maybe you are one of those whom teachers have labeled as a "late bloomer." This is the classic term describing a student who has ability but who, for some unknown reason, has chosen to keep that ability under wraps all the way through secondary school—at least until the college application essay has to be written. You know the type. Every class has one or more late bloomers. They do well on standardized testing, often they read a great deal, they are provocative in conversation, they generally have something intelligent to say on any topic, but choose not to engage in class discussion or perform up to their capacity on papers or exams. For some reason their security blanket has been intellectual immaturity, but teachers are beginning to detect a change. Do you know anyone like that? Maybe it's you. If so, you have a first-class opportunity to take your pen in hand and let that pent-up ability roll. Here is your chance to make a case for yourself. It may make the difference between acceptance and denial.

Convincing essays may make readers more interested. What you don't know is that admissions officers often think that the most interesting candidates are the "late bloomers." But they need some evidence to corroborate their gut feeling. A couple of well-written essays can help the reader who becomes your friend in court make a case for you in admissions committee deliberations.

Here are a collection of essays presented for your review with no editorial comment or grammatical corrections. They may help you with your thinking and give you some ideas on style and length. Some are titled and some are not. In your opinion, have they been proofread? If so, is it good proofreading? Maybe you could critique them on your own. Each essay could be improved. They are quoted verbatim, so what you see is exactly how they were submitted. By analyzing these, you will sharpen your editing tools when it comes to doing your own proofreading. The names of the authors have been withheld in deference to their confidentiality.

## THE MAN ON 96TH STREET

On the corner at 96th Street and Broadway there is a man who calls the doorway next to McDonald's home. He is a man of about forty. His hair is greasy; he wears a patch over his left eye, an eye which I imagine was destroyed in the Vietnam war; he has one leg and a stump where the other once was. On his left foot he wears a bag that acts as a shoe, and around his shoulders a ripped and ragged blanket shields him from the cold. If you listen carefully you hear a timid request, "Do you have any ex-

*(continued)*

tra change?" Hundreds of people pass him daily, most without even hearing his cry either because they are tuned to the latest music on their Sony Walkman or because the noise of construction work on the new luxury condominiums across the street is too loud, or the horns and cars, buses, and subways drown him out. Ironically it is technology that shields us from hearing or dealing with the most primitive problem, poverty. On school days I observe the problem only briefly, in transit between the comfortable suburb where I live and the private school I attend. I have become less able to ignore the problem because the man on 96th Street has become an individual to me.

One day I was hurrying to catch my train and bus home. The rush hour crowd was so thick on the corner of 96th, I was annoyed at the prospect of missing my train. The only way out of this gridlock of people was to step over the outstretched leg of the man on 96th Street. I did so. At least two other people followed in my path. I got to the train, but my conscience started to bother me. I was uncomfortable because I had just literally stepped over another human being. In my haste, I hadn't even dropped a coin into his cupped hands, which I often did to placate my feelings of guilt. The whole ride home I couldn't stop thinking about this man. I wondered if he had a family, how he lost his eye, and leg, and if he had friends. All of a sudden he wasn't just the man on 96th Street but a human being. I realized that society as well as myself is guilty of figuratively and literally stepping over a great many people. I thought about some efforts that had been made, shelters and soup kitchens, or the recently passed New York law allowing the homeless to vote as long as they give the nearest park bench or corner as their address. I also realized that my conscience could no longer allow me to overlook the man on 96th Street.

I called a nearby church to find out what services they offer for the homeless. They had none but referred me to St. John's Cathedral. They only had room for ten and said they were always full. There was another number to call and many after that. They would not come to him; he would have to go to them. I didn't know how to approach him, or whether he would even accept such services. The only thing I could think of to do was something personal. He nodded when I placed on his lap a package containing my father's old overcoat and shoes. This small gesture made me feel a little better but I don't even know if it did anything for him.

*(continued)*

I plan eventually, to go to law school. My goal is to be a lawyer who can provide services for the poor and homeless. I am embarrassed that I had to physically step over another person before re-evaluating myself and the society that I am caught up in. I know that there are many men, women and now families that live on corners around the country and I can not help them all. However, I hope to train myself to be an effective advocate for, at least, some of them. This quote by Edward Everett Hale best expresses my ideals:

"I am only one
But still I am one
I cannot do everything
But still I can do something
And because I cannot do everything
I will not refuse to do the something that I can do."

## UNTITLED

The issue that I have chosen to write about is of personal importance, but should be of national importance as well. The issue to which I am referring is the systematic destruction of the nation's high school seniors by College Essays. Nowhere on this application is there even an attempt at justifying the use of the dreaded Essay. Deans of Admissions everywhere are guffawing behind their huge oak desks at the pitiful submissions that otherwise promising candidates submit. It is high time that someone (or Someone) sees that this devastating tool be removed from the hands of colleges everywhere.

Oh, the admissions officers (a very militant title, isn't it) claim that these essays are legitimate tools of the whole process, but this claim is to be expected. You wouldn't, after all, expect to hear the truth about the circus from the ringmaster, would you?

When asked how they use these "legitimate tools" to facilitate the decision they answer promptly. "To examine the writing skills of the applicant to see if he will be able to survive the rigorous academic challenge at [insert school here]", rings the voice down from the mountain top on which the officers isolate themselves from the rest of us, who are not endowed with their omnipotence, the mortals.

This is almost as humorous as um . . . Nope, this is in a class by itself. Using an essay as one of the tools to determine the potential of a candidate is on par with having a

*(continued)*

Boy Scout (no, nothing is sacred) hike alone through the Rockies for two weeks to see if he is ready to go on his Troop's overnight in Johnny Hendrick's backyard.

It is highly improbable that the pressure felt during the application process will be duplicated in the first few years of college. In addition to the fact of giving needless gray hairs and ulcers to men and women in the prime of their lives, essays cause equally needless drops in grades and relaxation time. So instead of cultivating the fine young minds of America, colleges are turning this great land of ours into a land of gray-headed, Alka-Seltzer popping wasteoids (now there's a neat word).

"That is all extremely hypothetical; what is concrete is the grasp of the applicant's character that it gives Us." (I don't know how they do it but some people can get capital letters when they speak) (mostly admissions officers and politicians).

To refute this argument I offer myself as an example. By now I have probably come across as the type of person who makes people in general (admissions officers in particular) want to have a daughter so they could forbid her to marry me.

But I'm not all that bad. It's just that the essays are wreaking havoc at my school. Please, it must stop (okay, so much for the humanitarian plea).

I feel the only way to stop this hideous crime against us all is for all of the seniors to band together and do as I do, refuse to write your college essays.

And now, my purpose achieved, it's nap time. Goodnight.

---

### ME

I am not a joiner or a loner. Neither am I a follower. But I am not a leader, at least not in the common connotation of the word. I am not an actor or athlete, class president or drum major.

I fall into a unique category of leadership; I lead by setting a quiet example of independence and by observing people and noting minute details. Although I maintain a 3.95 grade point average and have been involved in student government and other clubs, my specific talent lies in writing. As past circulation manager and present copy editor and columnist for my school newspaper, I have had many opportunities to express myself to a

*(continued)*

large audience. As a journalist, I wrote one of the Nebraska High School Press Association's "Top Ten News Stories", an article presenting an unbiased view of a controversial amendment proposed to the state constitution.

But my heart lies in fiction. Last October I opened a letter from *Seventeen* magazine that I'd initially mistaken for a subscription plea. To my surprise, the contents of the envelope informed me that I had won Honorable Mention in their fiction contest. A year before, I had sent my manuscript without telling anyone; I didn't want anyone to be aware of my disappointment if it was rejected. As it happened, my story was nationally one of seven best out of 5000 entries. My secret effort paid off. This and other writing awards I have received have given me confidence in my writing talent, along with the respect of my classmates for the pursuit of an art that often seems to go unheralded.

Most recently I participated in the Arts Talent and Recognition Search (ARTS) in Miami, Florida, in the discipline of writing. Over 6000 students applied; one hundred and five were invited to Miami. I spent four days in the company of some of the most talented young people in the nation. I had the chance to share my passion for writing with other young artists as well as marvel at the genius of dancers, musicians, actors, and painters. Although I have taken the creative writing course offered at my school for two years, I had never met anyone so dedicated to their art, be it writing or another form.

Rather than a hobby, I consider writing a necessary part of my day and inherent part of myself. I spent this past summer dissecting literature, averaging three books weekly, from Ann Beattie and Tom Wolfe to Henry James and Leo Tolstoy. I own countless floppy disks full of plot ideas and potential characters, and manila folders full of completed stories awaiting my editing. I also exercise my poetic ability by writing and recording songs with my band, the "2 Ripe Bananas." My fellow Bananas and I are the proud authors of a rock opera ("Don't Put Those Bananas in the Freezer") and a complete album.

My love for the reading and writing of literature has led me to the decision to major in English, or creative writing if possible, in college. I enjoy both writing prose and poetry, and papers examining those things as well— the lines of e.e. cummings, the simplicity of Ernest Hemingway, the symbolism of George Orwell. Manipulating words, for me, is as integral to my survival as my heartbeat. I have the need to learn from the masters' manipulation how to perfect my own "literature."

*(continued)*

My peers appreciate my literary tendencies, and come to me if they don't understand Hamlet, need help phrasing a thesis statement, or can't remember into which species of dinosaur iambic pentameter is categorized. But they also come to see me if they need a Snoopy Band-Aid, if they can't recall the third line of "Mrs. Robinson," or if they want to know how Scooby Doo and Woody Allen illustrate the meaning of life.

While other leaders pound podiums, football fields, or the floorboards of a stage, I choose to lead, not silently, but with the quiet scratching of a ball-point pen.

## WHAT WOULD THE WORLD BE LIKE IF FOURTEEN YEAR OLD BOYS WERE IN CHARGE?

I have the feeling that if 14 year olds were in charge of this world, we would be in quite a bit of trouble, especially if my brother represents the typical fourteen year old. Older sisters of the world would probably be shackled in dark cellars, rock music would flood the streets and replace national anthems, school and homework would be outlawed, and t-shirts and jeans would become "formal attire," not to mention unbelievable changes in diet. The national problems that face us now would be dealt with in incredible ways.

Concerns for the environment would at best be minimal. Boys this age don't give much thought to toxic waste dumps or nuclear waste pollution, in fact, they rarely think much beyond what television show is on next. My experience has been that they do not even care what state of cleanliness their body, clothes, or room is in, unless if they are trying to impress someone. My brother's room would stand as evidence of this. Noise pollution would also become a desperate problem. Those huge radios, commonly referred to as boxes, would haunt everyone. At full volume, at all times, it wouldn't be long before the earplug industries were thriving.

With such an important issue as the economy, I don't know what would happen. Surely the fast food market would thrive, and massive spending on record albums, sports equipment, and mini bikes would occur. What, however, would become of fine foods, ballet, and orchestras? They would fade into the walls and join a long history of other forgotten treasures like the hula hoop and the twist. Yet would history be maintained, would we

*(continued)*

know what went on before us? My brother tends to forget how important it is to learn from past mistakes. He often repeats the same ones over and over again. Never realizing the consequences, fourteen year olds also love to gamble and live on credit, which would cause the Great Depression of the 1920's to be relived.

After they had destroyed the economy, they would begin on foreign policy, which would be a totally new game, literally. Not realizing the potential difficulties of their situation, they would not take world problems too seriously. On the other hand, if they did, it would probably be worse. The temperament of a boy this age as he passes through puberty is difficult to predict. A request to bring out the garbage often brings an angry retort. Imagine what would happen if he were asked to negotiate peace treaties with the Soviets. "I can't talk with them tonight; I'd miss my favorite TV show!" Different priorities would also prevail; the size of our defense department would probably not be as crucial as the size of our refrigerators. Instead of conventional means, the teens could have junk food eating contests or mini-bike races to settle international problems.

This may be an unfair judgment of fourteen year olds, and to the mature ones, I apologize, but this is my perception based on personal experiences. In addition, I would like to remind the youngsters who perchance may read this that they are not in charge. Also, my apologies go out to the people whose jobs may be jeopardized in this scenario: sanitation workers, teachers, violin players, etc. throughout the world.

## PERSONAL STATEMENT

*For several years now, I have programmed computer games in C. Like many game programmers, I sometimes imagine writing a computer game about myself. I believe the ideas behind this yet-to-be created game might offer some insight into who I am.*

## DIRECTIONS FOR "THE FRUITS AND VEGETABLES WITHIN"

The goal of the game: achieve a balance between Randy's activities with the fruits and those with the vegetables. Randy is the avocado seen on the introduction screen. To

*(continued)*

maintain that balance, schedule Randy's time so he can succeed as both an athlete and as a scholar. Although Randy enjoys the company of both groups, like all avocados, he prefers not to be classified entirely as a fruit or a vegetable.

In the scenes in the school newspaper's production room, you will quickly discover that Randy has the knowledge, understanding and leadership to work competently with the vegetables. In addition, Randy's work brings an exclusively avocado-ish creativity and perspective that most vegetables cannot offer because they have not experienced both fruit-and-vegetable-dom. Make sure that Randy retains that frame of mind or else he will become solely a vegetable.

If he is spending too much vegetable time, send Randy to take a jog or play ultimate frisbee, some of his favorite athletic pastimes. That will redirect the Fruit-Vegetable-Balance-ometer toward the fruit region.

When playing tennis, Randy's seriousness and determination set him apart from the other fruits. His strength is patient, smart playing as opposed to the brutish impulsiveness of many athletes. If you allow him to play too long, however, Randy will turn into a stereotypical dumb fruit and lose his ability to work effectively with vegetables. To help Randy recover from overexposure to fruits, you could have him read the Civil War book next to his bed or let Randy program a game on the computer. Programing is Randy's favorite vegetable activity because it challenges him to integrate his creativity and artistic abilities with his logic and mathematical skills.

In order to win, you must make the Fruit-Vegetable-Balance-ometer rest on the avocado marker. When you near that point, you may make fine adjustments by partaking in pastimes that are very close to perfect avocadoness. Juggling and hiking will move the meter slightly to the fruit zone and playing the harmonica will tip it into the vegetable region.

*It is fair to ask why I want to be a well-rounded avocado. I believe that balanced people are more interesting than lopsided individuals. A balanced person can take the best elements of the scholar and the best elements of the athlete and incorporate them into his personality, because he has experienced the lives of both.*

*Plato best explained this when he wrote, "He who is only an athlete is too crude, too vulgar, too much of a savage. He who is only a scholar is too soft, too effeminate. The ideal citizen is the scholar-athlete, the man of thought and action."*

## THE FINAL TEST

Stanley Albert Tukos waited patiently behind some twenty-odd people. He felt confused, almost as if he had been hit over the head. After what seemed like an eternity, Stanley reached the front and approached the heavy-set woman behind the desk. He stood in awe at the huge gate which lay behind her. It was bigger than anything he had ever seen. "Name?" she asked.

"Where am I?" Stanley asked, dazed at what lay before him.

"Listen, mister," said the woman, "I dont have all day. What's your name?"

"Stanley, Stanley Tukos, but where am I and why do you want to know who I am?"

"What a'ya, stupid or somethin'? You're in heaven. Let's see, Tukos." She opened a book thicker than any dictionary Stanley had ever seen. "Ah, Stanley Albert Tukos, you were hit by a car, weren't you?"

"I don't know," said Stanley. "Am I dead?"

"I see we have a real Einstein here. Of course you're dead. What do you think this is, a joyride?" Just then two men approached the desk. Both were dressed in three-piece suits and, with the exception of their wings, looked more like Wall Street business men than angels in heaven.

"Mr. Tukos, we've been expecting you," said the taller of the two. "We understand you're probably a little confused as to your whereabouts but don't worry, that's normal. In time you'll understand where you are and what you're doing here. In the meantime, my name is Malcolm, and my friend here is Harvey. Malcolm is not my real name, but, well, that's a long story. Maybe one day I'll tell you about it."

"I don't want to hear it. I just want to go home."

I'm afraid that's not possible. You see, we used to do that once in a while, y'know, send people back to earth, but it got kind of complicated. Some of them started remembering and appearing on TV shows like GOOD MORNING AMERICA. They even made a couple of movies like, what was that one called, HARVEY?

"BEYOND AND BACK," Harvey replied.

"Oh, yeah, well, it was bad publicity for us, so the Boss, who lives upstairs, kind of got upset."

"If this is heaven, said Stanley, "how come I didn't know I was dying?"

"It was very sudden," answered Malcolm.

*(continued)*

"Very sudden, repeated Harvey, "and don't get too cocky, you're not in heaven yet. This is only Heaven's gate."

"Oh," said Stanley, "Well, when do I get to heaven?"

"We have to know a little about you first," Malcolm answered, "Like why we would want you here in heaven. What have you accomplished?" Stanley began to grin.

"Well, sir, I invented the S.A.T."

"The who?" asked Harvey.

"The S.A.T., y'know, the Scholastic Aptitude Test. That's a very big deal back on earth. The test will either get a kid into college or keep him out. In other words, it separates the men from the boys."

"Y'know. I remember that test," said Harvey. "My son studied ten months for it and still ended up with a 1050."

"Oh," said Stanley. "I'm sorry to hear that. But think on the bright side, it's only his college education."

"You make a lot of kids miserable, y'know. We don't like that attitude here in heaven. Did you do any Advanced Placement work during your lifetime?"

"What kind of work is that?" asked Stanley.

"Like charity. things that get you in good with the Boss."

"No, not really," replied Stanley, looking very disappointed.

"I don't know. Stan," said Malcolm, "we might have to reject you."

Maybe not," said Harvey. "we'll see how you do on your Heaven Entrance Exam."

"Heaven Entrance Exam?" questioned Stanley. "That's not fair. I didn't have time to study. I didn't know I was going to die."

"That's all right, Stanley, you can't study for this. It's a piece of cake."

"But I didn't take the Kaplan course."

"Don't worry. you'll do fine. You can't study for this test," replied Malcolm. Stanley was then seated at a table and given a number of pencils. Three hours later, he finished and handed the test to Harvey. Harvey placed the exam in the computer and, in less than five minutes, returned with the results.

"Well, Stanley," says Harvey. "we have some good news and some bad news. The bad news is you got a 700 combined. The good news is we have a less competitive afterlife downstairs."

## UNTITLED

Women are property. Their feelings are insignificant. They are only useful for cleaning house, cooking, raising children, and most important of all, producing strapping sons. Women must not be consulted on consequential issues for they are meek and senseless. They must obey the head of the patriarch family. If they forget their place, show them who is in charge.

This is a common view among many Asian societies. It is an absolute dogma in the Hmong culture which has effected strife between my relatives (including my parents) and me. I refuse to accept this antiquated notion and have thus spent my adolescence trying to break out of the domesticated housewife mold and prove that I am not a worthless, burdensome daughter.

However, it is a difficult struggle. Sometimes I feel depleted of any strength to carry on my task. It is especially hard because everyone around me criticizes me for the tiniest things. There is always the social pressure of marriage. Many young girls are intelligent, but collapse under that pressure. If a girl is not married by age twenty, she is referred to as a spinster. Furthermore, Hmong men over twenty-five tend to marry teenage girls, rather than their contemporaries. With a bleak, lonesome future staring them in the face, most girls turn to marriage before it is too late. These women usually end up discovering that their hopes, dreams, and aspirations are lost because their husband did not see it fit for her to continue her education.

That is a tragic problem which confronts my generation. Teachers tell us that we can do anything we put our mind to, but for a Hmong girl, it takes extra work. If she does anything out of the ordinary, she is subject to criticism. A female can never do anything right.

And that is my dilemma. I am too outspoken for my family to handle. I will not conform to be the ideal Hmong woman because I cannot degrade myself to groveling for a man. They often accuse me of being insolent, but I respect my parents more than anything. It is just that I have ideas, beliefs, and values which I fight for. In addition, I am never given the credit I deserve.

When I received a scholarship to study at Oxford University this past summer, my relatives urged my parents to not let me go or else I will return pregnant and cause the family to lose face. Girls are not trusted. I have always told my parents of my whereabouts, but because I

*(continued)*

am a girl, I am prone to be a liar. If I receive straight A's, they tell me that I study too much and am negligent with my chores. This is quite contradictory considering the fact that I took over my mother's work around the house when I was 8-years-old. It is little things like this which pitted me against all my relatives.

However, there is yet another event I got involved in which truly angered my parents. Recently, there was a vote in St. Paul for the repeal of the gay rights act. I believe in equal treatment because I have seen what prejudices have done in my culture. I planned to go and demonstrate at the state capitol against repeal. I confided to my sister because I wanted her to understand the issue and I hoped she would grow up to be a person who would change the world. She became scared because the only protests she had seen were violent riots on television with police officers breaking up people and arresting them. She told my parents and they locked me in my room.

That night, I received a harsh lecture on the role of women. Prior to this, my parents and I were on good terms. We communicated fairly well, although they often got upset with my ways. My father threatened to disown me if I ever get myself jailed and disgrace the family. He is somewhat liberal, but still a staunch believer in family pride and the superiority of men. My mother, I am sad to say, does not think it is my role to be out there fighting for something irrelevant to me, but in actuality, it is. If someone is being mistreated, it is up to society to take responsibility. We have to come and rescue those who are crying for help or else we will stand alone in the end. I was angry at my parents' narrow view, but it was useless to try and reason with them. It will only give me a longer lecture. That is the way it is always like. After a few days, they will simply accept that I will not change and just keep a sharper lookout on me. Yet despite this friction between us, I still respect my parents and my culture even though it frustrates me to be treated so lowly.

On the contrary, this unjust treatment has been the sole driving force behind everything I do. I used to hate the Hmong culture because I felt trapped and restricted. I once thought it limited the scope of things I could do. Now, however, I feel proud and privileged to grow up in a strict, traditional family because it has strengthened me. Although women are treated like slaves, it makes success a little sweeter.

## UNTITLED

There are so many factors, events and conditions that affect a person's perceptions, and feelings; indeed, a person's values and future directions.

When I was sixteen years old something happened in my life that truly affected me. Something I would like to share. Like so many other teenagers, my life's concern centered around clothes, my hair, and being popular. These issues were important to me and my peers, but, I'm afraid, not particularly significant beyond our well protected environs. My family after all is upper middle class; my mother owns a nursery school and my father is a psychotherapist. We are comfortable, very close and talk often about things we think and care about.

One New Year's Day, my mother and I were talking about values and how they might change in the era of the 1990's. She thought the 1990's would be a time of "minimalism"; a period different from the 1980's when greed and self-centered behavior were the order of the times. My mother felt that this would be replaced in favor of greater social consciousness. As one might guess, I rather rejected her premise. After all, I thought, I'm not ready for "this"! I'm a teenager. I don't need to worry about my self-centered behavior and "minimization." My mother and I talked at some length and discussed ways to be more socially responsible in our personal commitments. Though reluctant, I agreed to try out my mother's "minimization and giving" lifestyle and decided to volunteer in a program to feed the homeless. I joined a program and was assigned to work once a month at a homeless shelter in Peekskill, New York.

I should mention, my parents are very generous people and I think I am as well, but feeding twenty homeless people on a Friday night when my friends were out having fun was not exactly my idea of the thrill of a lifetime, but I had made the commitment and I was bound and determined to follow through.

During the weeks leading up to Thanksgiving, a particularly busy time at the shelter, I had several conversations with an American Indian friend. He was very involved in the Indian movement and shared with me many of his cultural values. He told me about "Mother Earth" and gave me literature about the unjust treatment perpetrated upon Indians by greedy, self-centered people. He told me of the difficult life of the American Indian in the early time, and perhaps more importantly, to-

*(continued)*

day. He discussed with me his views on the "hypocrisy of Thanksgiving," which quite frankly evoked in me a sense of guilt. I thought, why should I celebrate a holiday that glorifies the mistreatment of the American Indian; mistreatment that continues even today. I decided that I would protest by not attending our traditional family Thanksgiving dinner at my grandmother's house. My parents were, predictably, supportive but insisted I call my grandmother personally to tell her that I wouldn't be at this year's Thanksgiving "celebration," and why. Though she was disappointed, she understood my motivations. As I said, my family is very close and comfortable with one another.

I was assigned to work at the shelter on Thanksgiving and arrived early in the morning to help prepare the traditional Thanksgiving meal. Though I often felt imposed upon when I had to work at the shelter, this day would be different.

Normally, the people who came to the shelter on Friday evenings were "regulars." The same faces; hungry men and women, often not very clean. This day, however, people were bussed in from surrounding communities. These people were just as hungry and some weren't very clean, but for the first time, I saw homeless children . . . young boys and girls clinging to their mothers, obviously fearful they would be suffocated in the noise and activity of the growing crowd, lost forever from the security of parental love and presence. It was frightening to see these lost and helpless people, and the impact was lasting.

The Thanksgiving meal was well organized. Ten persons were seated at a table. Two volunteers were assigned to each table to serve them. One volunteer would run back and forth to get food and drink while the other would sit and make conversation. I was a "sitter and talker," a specialty I've developed over the years. I circulated around the table trying to make people feel comfortable. Some responded politely while others looked with suspicion. I've often thought about their reaction and have concluded their suspicions were certainly justifiable. After all, why should they trust me? Why wouldn't they think I was "looking down" on them. There I was a preppie looking girl dressed in loafers, designer jeans and cardigan, complete with "GAP" labels.

As I walked my way around the table I came upon a rather frazzled looking black man. He was sickly, frail and wrinkled. His bones were visible through his skin. Obviously hungry, he enjoyed four platefuls while we

*(continued)*

talked. During an unguarded moment he stuffed food into his tattered army jacket, apparently thinking to his next meal. We enjoyed a long conversation. He reminisced about his youth, the Vietnam War, in which he fought, and about the difficulties of his life. I talked about my life and my family and about college. As we talked we became less guarded, more comfortable and understanding of one another. When, after several minutes, I asked if there was anything he needed, he replied simply, "All I need now is my family . . ." He grabbed my hand and repeated several times words I will never forget. He said, "Thank you for treating me like a person."

Walking to my car after everyone had left the shelter that evening I thought how easy it was and how good it felt to treat that man as a "human being." After all, isn't that what he is? Isn't that the way we should treat all people . . . with caring and compassion. Then I realized what had happened. I realized that it was that man who made me feel special. I had learned from him! I was moved, so moved I cried all the way home.

When I arrived at my house I ran up the front steps and called my grandmother to ask her to set one more place at the table. Perhaps there was something to celebrate after all. Perhaps I hadn't lost my interest in the welfare of others, but had simply learned to put that interest into perspective.

I never saw that man again. I think about him often, about that Thanksgiving, and I wonder if he's safe and well. I want to thank him for being such an important part of my life. I want him to know I care.

## DISCUSS SOME ISSUE OF PERSONAL, LOCAL, OR NATIONAL CONCERN AND IT'S IMPORTANCE TO YOU

It's two o'clock. The bell has rung, and in unison seven hundred teenage bodies head for their lockers to gather books, jackets and other belongings. In many ways they look the same: young, jean clad and relieved to be through another day of high school. On closer look, of course, there are really seven hundred individuals. The bodies could be separated in many ways—attractive and unattractive, tall and short, fat and thin. One difference, however, that seems to separate groups, a difference that should not be, is that some bodies carry home many

*(continued)*

books to be read and studied and cursed over for several hours later that night. Another group, a group far too large, leaves empty handed. How can this be? How can this latter group be ending the day at two o'clock? Has their academic day been such that they have no need to reinforce what they have learned during the day? Unfortunately, that is not the answer. The answer is that too many students in American schools are allowed to pass through four years of high school unchallenged, unmotivated, and unthinking, and are allowed to finish high school unprepared to challenge, motivate, or think when they get out. Many debate over how to solve the condition of American education. The teachers say that the answer lies in more money. The President says that the answer lies in school choice. They are probably right—these changes would probably help, but all anyone needs to do to see an even simpler solution is to stand in the halls of any high school at two o'clock and watch the empty handed students as they leave. A far simpler solution would then have to become as evident to them as it is to me: raise the academic standards.

One way to raise the standards would be to have teachers of all levels of courses, not just honors courses, make students work hard for grades of A or B. These grades should be reserved for those students who have worked hard and have done exceptional or good work in the subject. C's should be what they were originally meant to be—an average grade. Too often students, in non-honors courses, are given C's as a rule, even with D averages. C has come to mean failure, not average. Teachers should not be afraid to give out D's and F's. If anything it may make the student spend more time studying and therefore learning more.

Aside from making good grades harder to get, another way to raise academic standards would be to make the courses harder. There should not be a wide gap between what is expected, for example, in an honors physics class and what is expected in a standard physics class. Students in both sections should be made to reach. Bright students should be encouraged to take the most difficult courses that they can and not be allowed to coast, getting those good grades, in classes they could pass blindfolded. Homework should be mandatory in all classes. If a student claims that he got all of his work done in study hall, his courses are probably not challenging enough. No class should be a "Cliff Notes" class, where students can pass a test having only a bare bones knowledge. No

*(continued)*

classes should be spoon fed; students should have to work hard.

More meaningful grades and harder courses—these are easy ways to solve a serious problem. However the standards of education will never be improved unless we improve the standards for our teachers. There is something wrong with education when people who are good at teaching, like my father was, leave the profession. There is something wrong with education when teachers like my mother, who loves her job, discourages her own children from entering the teaching profession. I think teachers are discouraged because they are all lumped together—good and bad—in the eyes of most people. Because of this, teachers lack the same pride in their profession as others have in theirs. Who wants to admit that they went through four years of college and two years of graduate school to make an average to below average salary and to be looked down upon? How can this be changed? First of all get rid of all the poor teachers. Would the airlines keep a pilot who couldn't fly? Would a hospital keep a surgeon who no longer cared? Of course not. That is why we respect pilots and surgeons—we know that they have to meet certain standards. Let's not keep teachers who can't teach and who no longer care. Secondly, let's increase the pay of those who do a good job. This should be fairly simple to decide. There is not a kid in my school who could not name the five best and five worst teachers. If we can decide this, why can't the principal or some appointed board? If the better teachers were paid better salaries, then brighter college students would be drawn to the teaching profession. Once poor teachers were eliminated, salaries were raised, and the profession became associated with the best minds, then teaching would be a profession to be proud of. Kids could only gain.

I know that there are many problems facing America today. As a senior in high school, these problems are soon to become my problems. I know none of them have an easy solution, but it seems to me that education could be improved by simply improving our standards.

## PERSONAL STATEMENT

My earliest memory (I think) is red. I can see through a haze of some kind, and what I see is a red, nearly translucent, warm, soft and rounded wall; there is a low and very comforting noise in the background. I'm afraid this isn't an "honest" memory, though. I think I deliberately remembered it just to spite someone who said it wasn't possible.

My memories come in images after that. I see clear as yesterday a picture of the sun setting over the white sand beach of Puerto Vallarta, or the ocean spray on the ferry to Guadalupe, or the seagreen smiling plastic octopus that hung over my favorite shopping center in Guadalajara. I even have a picture from a childhood dream: I am on a three-colored beach, with my mother and my car, watching a tsunami towering above us. But these are only pictures: all I do is see them there in my mind, I can't touch them and they do not affect me except insofar as to make me say, "Oh yes; I was there too."

The first real memory I have, more like a movie than a photo album, is of Maine. I have many images of Maine, as well: I can see a tree, in the middle of an otherwise empty lot, a hundred feet tall and dead as a wooden chair. I see myself playing on the twelve foot wide stump after they cut it down. But these images, too, lack the emotion of a real memory.

When I was five, or a little under that age, I was delivering "Meals On Wheels" as a volunteer. I remember near-endless sterilized hallways, of white or off-white, and ochre ceilings and checkerboard black-and-white institutional floors, and the green doors with the little painted numbers on each of them; behind each of them, a chair, a single bed, a sink, and a bath, and another old lady or man. I remember one in particular. She must have been over ninety; I do not remember her name. She was once married. She had children, none of whom ever came to visit her. She used to love to touch my white, curly hair, white like hers but thick where hers was so thin you could see nearly through to her skull. I remember going into her room, day after day, and seeing the same things: her blue shawl, hung off the back of a wooden chair; a brightly colored cardigan she would try to knit when her arthritis wasn't too bad, but it was bad most of the time; her bed, always half-made, so when she sat up for us to give her her meal, it was in doubt whether she had been asleep or not; and I remember the stench.

*(continued)*

Her room smelled of too many cats over the years, of dust and wet leaves in the autumn, but a sweet, a sickly odor, also: like a forgotten wound, left to rot. I hated her for smelling that way, for making me smell that stench every day; I hated her for being so fragile, and like a hollow-boned bird, too easy to break. I hated her for touching my hair, when she didn't ask, and I had to act nice to her; and for being old and ready to die when all my world was fresh, new. I remember one day when I came into her room, and she was so happy to see me she broke into a huge smile: broke, literally, because her dried lips cracked and bled, and she didn't seem to notice. I was so revolted that I had to leave the room and wait outside.

I don't think I saw her after that day. I don't remember seeing her after that, but I may have. But I can't forget her face from that day: looking into the milky voids that once were her eyes, seeing for the first time the human face that was hidden underneath her wrinkles, and it came to me that those bleeding lips once kissed, that her eyes might have once looked upon a world that was as new as mine, and that her once-new world is now dust; and one day, my horrified mind concluded, mine would be, too.

## UNTITLED

Evaluate a significant experience or achievement that has special meaning for you.

The most significant achievement of my life has been to survive my father's mid-life crisis. At the age of forty-four my father decided that he needed a change. He resigned his position as priest of an Episcopal church and began a search for the "what next."

My father, however, needed a lot of daily support during this time and because Mom worked, I got the job. For three years I suffered with each new idea. He studied CO-BOL and I told him how wonderful his program was. If his program wouldn't run then I told him how marvelous he was. I went around the block when walking was "in" and drove for ice cream when it wasn't. I learned or maybe was forced to learn how to live with someone experiencing a significant change. That is my greatest achievement.

# The Ultimate Falsehood 10

There is a perception among too many people who should know better regarding the relationship between verbal scores and the ability to write. The perception is that low verbal scores equal poor writing. In fact, no one—including the College Board and the administrators at ACT—has ever made any claims that verbal scores in any of the recognized standardized tests are a measure of one's ability to write well.

If you are afflicted with a low verbal score (let's say in the 400s), and you are worried that the essay requirement will, therefore, "do you in," you may take comfort in the following essays written by young men and women, all of whom have either verbal SAT's or English composition scores in the 400s. Judge for yourself whether you think this is good writing. Based upon the following essays, is the relationship in question a myth or a reality?

## SHORT PEOPLE

I declare, for now and for all of eternity, the institution of international Short People's! We, the short, the small, the petite, and the genuinely tiny, hereby unite at the front of the line and cast off such demeaning impediments as "high heel" and "elevator" shoes. We are elevated; we are no longer the downtrodden and underfoot people we once were. We shall not be stepped upon; we rise as one unit under God to seek new heights of recognition and to further our many accomplishments in the arts, in the law, the government, and philanthropic society as a whole. We see in such giants as Napoleon Bonaparte and Toulouse Lautrec, the will and genius, the determination and drive, to make the world recognize our desire to be acknowledged in our true perspective. Others, such as the abbreviated Danny DeVito, famous twin of the olympic Schwartzenegger, show us that shortness can overcome the odds imposed upon us by society. We, the Short People of the world, raise our expectations and look to the stars. We are the stars and we are often . . . and rightly . . . looked up to.

Short People never look down their noses on anyone, any place, or anything. Short People are down-to-earth; they always look into the heart of the matter and usually speak to it through someone's belt buckle. This is evident by a four-fold increased risk of heart attacks among Short People. Short People care about everything. They are close to the ground and close to the really important things in life. Our national holiday, geared at letting others recognize our place in society, will give us the opportunity to 'stand up and be counted.' We are uplifting; we now need to be uplifted! We have raised a national consciousness and need to be given eye-to-eye appreciation for our heroic efforts. Short People have overcome a lot, for they had a lot to overcome. We are the true heroes and heroines of this world, for we try harder, work more, and jump farther to get ahead.

Short People are compressed into one space, but they are never abridged in thought and deed. They may be compact, but they are never compacted. National Short People's Day will commemorate me and all my short friends. We are the dynamite that comes in small packages; it is time to burst out of our packages and make ourselves felt in this world. Our champions are many: there is Dr. Ruth, F. Lee Bailey, and the Littlest Angel. Tinkerbell has taken us through Neverland and we have visited

*(continued)*

the Lilliputians along the way. We have only one thing to ask before we establish this glorious festival of compactness: we want the world to know that we may be short, but we have no "short" comings! Short People Day will occur in February, the shortest month of the year. Since I was born on February 3rd, I suppose I was predestined to be short. But, I shall look upon my birthright as a good omen, I was bound to be short, but I was never bound to be shortened.

## UNTITLED

"No matter what they take from me, they can't take away my dignity." Whenever I hear Whitney Houston sing this song, my heart sinks. It is my story. My battles, my struggles through a neverending divorce, paralyzed my family and taught me some survival skills.

> I believe the children are our future,
> teach them well and let them lead the way.
> Show them all the beauty they possess inside.
> Give them a sense of pride, to make it easier.
> Everyone is searching for a hero,
> Everyone needs someone to look up to.

Abruptly awakened by the vociferous roars and screeches, sometimes in the middle of the night, I could hear my parents, the contenders. Fatigued by their redundant and relentless battles, I decided to take refuge under my blankets. Yet, as hard as I tried to shut my eyes and to muffle the sound with my pillow, I could not ignore the sound of their vengeful voices. I reluctantly dragged myself out of bed, attempting to do the impossible, mediate the fight. Trying to pacify things, I played the referee in between two people who sought to drag one another to the depths of the deep cruel sea. As they were screaming and yelling cruel and harsh threats to one another, I was humiliated to think that these were supposed to be the people I revered the most. Also, terrified to think that the neighbors would be wakened by their bickering, I ran through the house shutting all the windows. At the same time, my heart went out to my poor younger brother who was blocking the garage door so that my mother could not leave. Once she was out there, I prayed that she was not out somewhere taking her life.

*(continued)*

Yet, the greatest difficulty came along with being in the middle of the warfare. Trying to appease both sides, it became difficult when one would say, "If you have such an easy time agreeing with your father, why don't you go live with him?" Or, the other one would say, "Why can't you tell me that I am right and show me that you are on my side, like your brother?" Trying to remain neutral, it became a difficult task when they were tugging at my heart from both sides. This is where I sympathize with children. Having my own share of being heart-broken, confused, and insecure by the evasive and dynamic ways of the world, I would like to try to make a better surroundings for future generations. Because of my experiences when I was younger, I would like to help the children realize that they are not alone. By studying deeper into their psychology I feel that I will have a better idea of what they feel and how they work. In my eyes, children possess an infectious sense of joy that brings a smile to my face. They also have the great capacity to love whether it be giving or receiving. It is not fair when their innocent worlds of marshmallow clouds or peppermint castles are destroyed. There are a lot of children calling out for help, wanting to try and find the light at the end of the tunnel. We, being the people they look up to, should make it easier for them to feel safe and secure.

Compelled to help simple and naive minds to survive in an intricate and enigmatic world, by taking my acquired strength and vitality, I can go a long ways.

## UNTITLED

When I was five years old, my favorite song was "My Life." by Billy Joel. That is pretty ironic considering that my lives began at age five when my parents got divorced. My life until eighth grade consisted of spending weekdays with my father and weekends with my mother. While that may seem like one life, it was actually two. My father, with whom I lived during the school week, was the disciplinarian. He and my stepmother made it clear at a very young age that school was very important, maybe even the most important thing in my life. Good grades and manners were expected. Because I went to such a small school with very few kids in my class, I was sort of an outcast because I was brought up very strictly. All this ended Fridays at 4 P.M. when I

*(continued)*

went to my mother's. My mother's house, swarming with lots of little step-siblings was practically the opposite. There was no discipline, no one watching over my shoulder to make sure my math problems were right, or that I was sitting up straight. These were definitely two different lives. As I got older, I felt frustrated by the fact that I couldn't spend time with my friends on weekends because, although my life was supposed to be "my time," weekends were really my mom's time. If I wasn't with her, her feelings were hurt. I also felt frustrated that I couldn't stay late at my mom's on a Sunday night. My dad picked me up at 4 P.M. and if I wasn't there, his feelings were hurt. It was around then that I learned that no matter what decision I made, someone's feelings would be hurt and it would never be the right one.

In ninth grade, another life began when I moved with my father and family to New York. Although I was sad at the thought that I could not see my mother every weekend, I was excited by the opportunity to meet new friends and not have to worry about whose house I was supposed to be at. Well, ninth grade came and went and I found myself again wrapped up in schoolwork, frustrated and overwhelmed by the size of the school and the competition among students to do well.

High school started, and besides occasional days when everything goes wrong, it has probably been one of the best times of my life. I feel like high school has helped me put a balance in my life. While schoolwork has always been my number one priority, maybe it's wrong to say this, but now it is number one tied along with about three other things: theater, my friends, and my family.

When I was in eleventh grade, my step-mom was accepted into Yale Law School. While at first it sounded great, lots of money in the future, no one to tell me to sit up straight or read a book, I didn't realize the additional stress it would create. She spends weekdays at school and comes home for most weekends. I learned that when dad comes home from work, he doesn't always feel like making dinner or running the vacuum. He can't do everything. As a result, these last two years have been kind of stressful for me. In addition to worrying about schoolwork, SAT's, colleges, and if any guy in the world will ever like me, I often find myself worrying about what we can make for dinner, whether I remembered to unload the dishwasher, whether someone remembered to feed the dog, when I'm going to have time to do my ironing, whether my little brother is doing O.K. in school, what

*(continued)*

kind of mood my parents will be in, and naturally remembering to tape "Beverly Hills 90210" every Thursday night. While this may sound like I'm making myself out to be the 1991 version of Cinderella, that is not true. It's just taking stock of those little additional stresses in my life.

There are, however, some great pleasures in my life. Backtracking a little, when I was in third grade I had my first on-stage experience in the theater. I was the only munchkin with a speaking part in our local high school's production of *The Wizard of Oz*. Since then, theater has played a large part in my life. I have always gotten some type of high from the theater, whether acting, backstage, or just watching. It has always been something that has made me very happy. I don't know why, maybe because when you're on-stage, there is a chance to show your true self through another character. In a part, you can always put a little bit of your real self into that character without anyone saying that it is wrong. You can get on stage and make people laugh or cry. You don't have to worry about the choices you are making and the feelings you are hurting. It's a chance to be free, to be yourself and have people applaud you for it.

Despite all of the frustrations of the admissions process, I am very excited about going to college. I see it as the opportunity of my life, and for my life: where I can study because I want to, not because someone is making me; where I can worry about whether or not I have enough quarters to buy a pizza instead of worrying about whether or not I remembered to defrost the chicken before I left for school; where I can make choices about my life, be they right or wrong, and not worry about whether it is the best one for my brother and sister, but instead, what's best for me, regardless of whose feelings are hurt—what I want. It's going to be my time, not my mom's or my dad's, my time, "My Life." As Billy Joel put it, "I don't need you to worry for me 'cause I'm all right. I don't want you to tell me it's time to come home . . . It's my life." If in college I can achieve this independence for which I have worked so hard, it will be the greatest applause I've ever received.

## UNTITLED

For me, teenage pregnancy is not a social problem. It is a personal one. So far this year, three of my friends have come to me fearing they are pregnant. Each time I have listened to the situation and tried to help come up with solutions. But inside, I'm exploding! I feel so sad and angry and scared all at the same time.

My sadness is perhaps better expressed as empathy. All you need to do is look at the face of a girl who's telling you she may be pregnant and you'll understand. The good front and even jokes from my friends are so transparent I can see the fear and conflicting joy and sorrow within them, and it nearly brings tears to my eyes. I know that no one my age is equipped to deal with this kind of emotional and physical upheaval, but that doesn't make it go away. And so sometimes, when I'm alone, I cry for my friends.

Yet, between my tears, I get angry. It's impossible and futile for me to be mad at my friends, so my rage focuses on the society they, and I, live in. My high school has offered me nothing in the way of education about obtaining and using birth control. How are we supposed to avoid pregnancy, much less AIDS, if the only message we get is: "Just say no"? Yes is so much easier and so much more common. Yet, even if condoms and birth control pills were handed out at the door, the problem would not be solved. Our society encourages spontaneity and "go with the flow." Most importantly, we can't *plan* our sexual encounters! As a teenager, and a woman, I'm not even supposed to think about sex until the moment is upon me. If I attempt to obtain birth control, then I must be asking for sex. And on top of everything else, nothing is handed out at the door. Actually, laying my hands on pills becomes difficult and expensive. Even buying condoms can be risky in this town where everyone knows everyone else and news travels fast.

And so, I'm terribly, terribly frightened. If one of my friends *is* pregnant, what will she face? The pain and loss of an abortion or the pain and ridicule and loss of being seven months along and a senior in high school. What a choice! Others in my school have had rumors of pregnancy circulate about them. How many more are facing what I'm watching my friends face? But what scares me the most is that nothing will change. Sure, one of them may go on the pill, and another will keep condoms in the secret compartment in her purse. But one will just go back to the

*(continued)*

method of telling her boyfriend, "Don't cum inside me." No one will change my school's policy, so Lisa won't be the last to have her friend buy an e.p.t. test at the local Wal-Mart. No one will make thinking ahead commonplace.

I'm one of the "lucky ones." I have parents who always talked to me about sex and let me go on the pill when I asked for it. What can I do for my friends? I wish I could lend them my parents. As it is, I listen. I buy the e.p.t. I make the doctor's appointment and hold their hand through it. I tell other friends to use birth control. This can't be a social issue for anyone. Jessie could be your daughter—Lisa, the next applicant. Beth could even be me.

## UNTITLED

College application—"Because your qualities as an individual are as important to us as your accomplishments as a student, what would you like us to know that you have not been able to share with us?" Where would I even attempt to begin with such a question? Significant moments that have made a special impact on me, milestones, goals for the future, all of this would not really cover the question. Essentially, the college is asking what significant features I consist of. Yet, that is just it, it is each minute detail that formulates me—however significant or insignificant it may appear to the reader. "For self is a sea boundless and measureless (p. 61, *The Prophet*)." "To measure you by your smallest deed is to reckon the power of the ocean by the frailty of its foam (p. 93, *The Prophet*)." So, what is one to do . . .

Our family has raised German Shepherds, and collected dolls from all around the world. Once, I was roller skating around the cars in our garage and, Beau, our dog at the time, chased me around the Chevy and bit my butt. Most of my life has been spent in a rural town on an outer island. It was an hour's drive to the only movie theater on the island, and it was there I spent each birthday, each year. One year I filled all the shoes in the house with my mom's maxi-pads thinking they were shoe cushions, and would remove some of their odors. Even my older brother, who was quite displeased, could not contain his laughter at my innocence. He has one arm, and it has affected everyone else in the family as well. When I got to the seventh grade, I entered Punahou, and ironically,

*(continued)*

chipped my tooth by tossing the dog's water dish high in the air, and forgetting to catch it. I, too, went through being concerned with fashion, and preoccupied with other's opinions. Now, I enjoy art—the curves and indentations of wood especially turn me on. Travelling is my number one priority—there are more countries I want to visit than not (far too many to list). After seeing the documentary firm *Suleiman: The Magnificent,* I was determined to learn the Arabic language, and study sixteenth-century Turkish art and culture. I detest onions, and prefer a bit of lemon in my tea. After seeing the movie *A Room with a View,* a romance based on E. M. Forster's novel, I was determined to run away with Mr. George Emerson myself. Like everyone else, I, too, welcome sunrises and sunsets, the aroma of wild flowers, vast fields, spectacular mountains, stretches of ocean, comfort and security. Dancing in warm rain, going to clubs, being among trees, and photography are among my special hobbies. I once took a course in sewing, and created what one might consider a pair of shorts. My picture of an ideal day would probably include a nice stroll to the nearest art exhibit (contemporary or classical), munching on fresh French bread with Rondele or Alouette, swigging orange juice all the while. I am for Capital Punishment, but Abortion is not as clear cut an issue—rape obscures everything. Truman Capote is my author for all times, Nadine Gordimer coming in a close second (at least, that is, for this five minutes). Blonde and blue-eyed as I am, I abhor chemistry—I long for Cappucinos at dawn, afternoon poetry, and Andy Rooney. My favorite town (so far) is Chicago—it's New York with that midwestern homey feeling. I seem to have many aspirations, yet I am the one left programming the VCR. I don't wear a watch, but manage to be on time, and no, I don't have a favorite color.

# What the Pros Think

In the early spring of 1992, forty seasoned and time-tested veterans of the admissions wars from across the country were invited to submit their thoughts on the college application essay. They were given the freedom to say what they thought—to call a spade a spade. They represent both the college and secondary school viewpoints. Here are some of the responses, all direct quotes:

*William K. Poirot*
*College Counselor*
*Brooks School*
*North Andover, Massachusetts*

Most seniors are not going to write great essays, at least not ones that will by themselves get the reader admitted. In fact, I know of college studies in which 3 percent of the essays helped the applicant, 2 percent hurt the applicant, and 95 percent, while perfectly respectable, had no effect whatsoever on the admissions decision. Yet I have seen even good writers crippled by the pressure they put on themselves to write a great essay, one that will get them admitted. I would like to mention some of the more common mistakes seniors make in deciding upon an essay topic, and in writing the essay.

First, don't write an essay that anyone of a thousand other seniors could write, because they probably will. By the nine-hundred and forty-second time a college person reads about how bad you felt after losing the big game, that essay has lost its emotional impact. You can write about losing the big game, but when you have finished, read it and ask yourself if anyone else could have written the same essay. If you think the college might receive even one other essay like yours, rewrite it. The fact that you cried after losing the big game doesn't distinguish you from all the others who might write this essay. On the other hand, the details—where you cried, who talked to you, exactly what you were thinking—probably will set you apart.

I think you should avoid writing an essay that will embarrass the reader. While you definitely must risk something personally in order to write an effective essay, the risk should not place a burden on the reader. The reader is not your therapist, not your confessor, and not your close friend. If you place the reader in any such role, he or she will be uncomfortable. You certainly want your essay to stand out from the crowd, but it is probably better to be forgotten than to be remembered in a negative manner.

Don't try to sell yourself. The college will exercise its quality-control function using the grades and scores, not the essay. They use the essay to flesh out the numbers, to try to see and hear the person in the application. Rather than persuading the college that you are great, just show them who you are, what you care about, what moves you to anger, what the pivotal points in your life have been so far.

Also don't try to write an important essay . . . the definitive statement on the Middle East crisis or on race relations in America. These essays tend to come across as much more pompous than their authors intend, I suppose because it is unlikely that a high school senior is going to make the definitive statement on a major topic. More to the point, these essays tend to be written from a detached, objective point of view, exactly the opposite of what most college people are looking for in an applicant's essay. They read your essay to find out who you are. When they want an informed opinion, they will go to the editorial pages, not their files of college essays.

Don't set out to write the perfect essay, the one with a huge impact, the one that will blow the doors to the college open for you. It just doesn't happen very often. It is largely a fantasy, and you will be putting enormous pressure on the still-developing writing skills of an eighteen-year-old. Think instead of giving the reader a sample of yourself, a slice of the real you, a snapshot in words. It doesn't have to be an award-winning photograph, it just needs to be really you and reasonably well focused. Imagine that if you wrote the essay next month, it might well be completely different, because you would be different by then. I find regularly that the best essays I read are the result of a concentrated forty-five minutes, not the result of hours and hours of agonizing.

I will give one caveat on the writing itself. Don't have others edit it and correct it until you cannot hear your own voice any more. Certainly, you should correct the spelling. Of course, you should rewrite the essay, probably several times. My favorite writer on the subject of writing, William Zinsser, has convinced me that there is no such thing as good writing, only good rewriting. Rewrite to make sure that your words are saying what you intend them to say. That is all. That is the primary goal of rewriting. Word choice and word order must remain yours: even if a more experienced writer might suggest the more precise word, it will not be your word and you will begin to disappear from the essay. And remember that the only reason this essay has for existing is to show the reader who you are.

Finally, relax. Your chances of writing an essay that gets you admitted when you otherwise would not have been are unbelievably remote. Pick something you feel strongly about, for that will give the reader a window into your heart, and just write it. Think of the choice of subject and the first writing as simply sharing some part of yourself with a new friend. This is not usually painful. The work should come in the rewriting stage.

Good luck.

*William R. Mason*
*Director of Admissions*
*College of the Holy Cross*
*Worchester, Massachusetts*

My feelings about the college essay are strong and represent a two-bladed sword. On the one hand I don't feel the myriad of national tests nor the transcript grades begin to tell us about a young person's writing skills. Especially from the point of view of a liberal arts college and its faculty those skills are extremely important when considering a candidate for admissions. The essay authored by a candidate then, can be extremely revealing of a student's basic writing skills, ability to think in complex ways, basic understanding of the principles developing an essay, and can be revealing of higher order thinking skills. Of course those applicants who are beginning to develop a true writing "voice" stand out among their peers. I think it's fair to say that the essay can provide us with tangible evidence of whether or not a candidate seems to be ready to learn in the liberal arts mode.

At the same time there has been much national publicity about the importance of an essay in this process including the *Yale Guide to Essay Writing* that sometimes I wonder whether the author is the applicant. Probably none of us will have the opportunity to determine whether the essay is written by the candidate, but my feeling is that most high school seniors are not devious and we have to trust the items they submit.

*Susan Case*
*College Counselor*
*Milton Academy*
*Milton, Massachusetts*

A sample of our packet on do's and don'ts follows:

General Guidelines:

Type or word process or very neat handwriting

Length—conform to guidelines; one page single spaced or two pages double spaced

Use your own voice—informal, conversational

Avoid humorous essays unless you are good; but freely use humor

Watch spelling

Avoid overly familiar quotations or definitions

Travelogues, Outward Bound, Mountain School, Death—need a personal, fresh perspective; any topic can work

Don't repeat lists of activities

Don't let mom or dad write it

Dialogue works

Think small—anecdotes and rich details work

Be free with format

Don't write about writing, SAT's or the college process

Accentuate the positive—even in a painful experience

Don't write a traditional introductory paragraph

The first few sentences are critical

The five paragraph essay is too repetitive

Goals of the Essay:

To help the reader get to know you—a window on your personality, values, goals

To illustrate your uniqueness

To enable the reader to evaluate your writing

To help the reader create a full (and hopefully memorable) picture of you

How to Write:

Decide your message first

Write as if you are brainstorming—then revise it

Spend as much time thinking as you do writing

If you are stuck, have a brainstorming session with someone close to you

If you write about an activity or an experience, focus not on how good you are or what you have accomplished, but what it means to you

Don't ask yourself or anyone else "What should I write about?"

The appropriate question is, "What should I tell them about me?" Reorganize your thinking

Test the "success" of your essay by asking someone to read it and then asking NOT "Do you like it?" BUT "What do you think it says about me?"

Finally, ask yourself, "If college deans were to place me with roommates based on this essay, would they be able to choose compatible people? Would it give them enough to go on?"

*Robert S. Magee*
*Director of Admissions*
*Indiana University*
*Bloomington, Indiana*

Only a small fraction, probably 20% or less, of freshman college applicants are required to write an essay and it is probably just as well. The sad, well-known truth is that much of American secondary education does not emphasize or teach writing. The students who are exceptions to this statement are lucky indeed.

As an admissions officer, I have worked in settings where an essay was required and where an essay was not required. My own view, developed over the years, is one of skepticism for the following reasons:

1. I believe that if an essay is a significant factor in the admissions screening process, it will work to the disadvantage of those students who have not had the opportunity to adequately develop writing skills.

2. I discover that I am increasingly cynical about some of the essays I read. Did the student really write it or was there a paid consultant involved in the development of ideas, the suggestion of phrases, the rewriting, or even the entire essay? Or was the essay developed within a class context in school, requiring numerous rewrites and amendments? While this is good writing practice, will this student have the self-discipline to write at the same level independently?

For the above reasons, I feel that the essay is less appropriate for the public institution which seeks to serve a cross section of its population. In such cases, many institutions will use a "live" writing sample, produced by the student during orientation/registration programs, as a means of placement into an appropriate writing course.

As an instructor of writing for many years, it has been my privilege to occasionally speak to high school students about "the essay." I have no major formula but often share ideas such as the following:

1. The essay should observe the basic rules of good writing. It should be highly readable, flow from one idea to another in a logical, easy to follow pattern, observe the basic rules of English grammar and composition,

and use as few words as possible. This involves the basic steps of idea development, any necessary research, good organization (a concise outline), writing of a first draft, and ample time to edit and rewrite.

2. Write about something that is important to you. If your topic is not important to you, it will not be important to the reader.

3. In developing an idea, sometimes it is helpful to list what in your mind are your two or three greatest accomplishments. This isn't as easy as it sounds and you should give yourself a number of weeks to develop the list and reflect upon it.

4. Many students write about their triumphs. How many have the maturity and the courage to write about their defeats and losses? A young woman wrote a very moving essay on the slow and painful loss of her beloved elder brother to AIDS. I suspect that the writing of this essay served as a valuable catharsis for her and it told the admissions committee volumes about her strength and sensitivity as she agonized through the long process in which the family faced pain, economic burden, community ostracism, self-doubt, personal fear of the disease, and, ultimately, the brother's death.

5. Lastly, and most importantly, try to distance yourself from your essay and put yourself in the place of the reader. Is the essay balanced? Does it present all of your feeling, thoughts? Does it accurately portray what you wish to say?

Like the development of an athletic or musical skill, the ability to write competently takes time, effort, criticism, suggestion, encouragement. In spite of the electronic age, the power of the written word has not diminished. Those who have the discipline to develop this ability will be in the minority but they will find that the ability to write is applicable in an amazing number of professions, occupations, and situations.

*Dodge Johnson*
*Educational Consultant*
*Malvern, Pennsylvania*

Of all the jobs involved in applying to colleges, writing essays turns more students to jelly than any other.

A sterling essay probably won't catapult you into a college your record doesn't justify. But if you're a "possible admit"—one of the "maybe's" of whom the college will take some but not all—it can thrust you ahead of the pack.

College essays aren't English themes. They must be well written, but good writing is not the object—nor is proving you "read the book" or even, believe it or not, psyching out what colleges want and giving it to them . . . They're opportunities to let admissions committees hear you speak with your own voice, to catch the flavor of what makes you special.

This kind of real-world writing often comes hardest to students whose college dreams are entwined with ivy but who have little curiosity. Typically, they garner top grades by giving teachers what they want rather than grappling with ideas. Their history papers win A's and B's as models of form but lack imagination, insight, and above all, fire.

When admissions officers curl up to read, they have no preconceptions of what your essay should say—any more than they know exactly what they're looking for when they shop for a dress or a sports jacket. As with clothes, they seek good design, expert tailoring, attention to detail, colors that work. But they "buy," because an essay reflects a thoughtful person of promise they'd love to make part of their college.

If the real "you" shines through, you'll be someone admissions officers would like to know rather that just another piece of paper. So when the Common Application, accepted by more than a hundred colleges, invites you to "evaluate a significant experience or achievement that has special meaning to you," choose an event because it matters to you, not because it's flattering or earth-shattering . . .

Set the scene. Let a mosaic of significant detail carry your story. Let your insights reveal your depth and quality. You don't have to be a genius to write good college essays. Most of us aren't. The key ingredient is time, something anyone can provide—for thinking subjects through, for craftsmanship achieved through successive drafts, for care with detail.

*Penny Oberg*
*Counselor*
*Horace Greeley High School*
*Chappaqua, New York*
*Writing in the NYSACAC newsletter, Winter 1991*

This is the time of year when college admissions people close their doors and read applications. On the rare occasions they emerge, the frequent first comments are, "These essays are terrible" or "Why can't kids write as well as they speak!" Instead of re-examining American secondary education, I'd like to suggest a different remedy—**ask better questions.** The questions which many colleges ask force 17 year olds to think like 40 year olds, have little to do with the reality of the struggles of adolescence, and are ones which you would never ask in an interview. No wonder they don't tell you what you want to know. Some samples:

1. If you were given an opportunity to spend the evening with one person, whom would you choose?

2. Write p. 217 of your autobiography.

3. Describe your closet.

4. What is ethical behavior?

5. Describe a situation when your ethical beliefs were questioned by someone you admired.

6. What idea has most influenced your life?

Who makes up these questions? Do colleges hire consultants, are they done by committee, or is there an admissions specialist who is assigned this task?

It seems to me that what colleges are trying to find out in the essay is something about the candidate's writing ability, and a little about her thought process. The most selective schools undoubtedly use the essay as a test for the cream's ability to rise to the top. (The fat content does increase, however.)

The **real issues** for 17 year olds revolve around a struggle for identity, a place in a peer group, independence from their parents, validation, success in school, and freedom from boredom. The ethical dilemmas they face concern sex, and to a lesser extent, drinking, cheating and loyalty. Even the brightest kids have trouble articulating that. Most can't pinpoint a significant experience—kids think that means a death of a friend or parent, or some handicap.

Friends mean everything to high school students—whether they have them or don't. But when an essay is written about how important a friend is, we all snicker. All my admissions friends are bored with essays about trips to Europe—so am I. But, for the suburban, mostly white, affluent kids I deal with, sometimes that first experience with beggars, or art in the open instead of a museum-Mom-made-me-go-to, is truly a serendipitous moment. The first time one realizes the world is not made up of all me's is truly a beginning. One of my admissions friends talks passionately about adolescents finding and writing in their own voice. It's a wonderful phrase; it sounds so adult. Adolescents don't have a voice—it's changing and for most, very silent when talking to adults. Admissions officers may be young to me, but to high school kids you are old. We are dealing with kids for whom the problem of what to do Saturday night and how to stop pollution are on the same scale—depending upon the time of day.

Help us out by asking more simply—tell us about you. Use these statements as a test. Remember who you were at 17; think about the best interviews you've had; try to answer your own college's questions, or ask a colleague to do so. Think about how you would feel if I asked you to answer your questions. The best way to get good honest answers is to ask good, honest questions.

*Francis B. Gummere, Jr.*
*Dean of Admissions*
*Lake Forest College*
*Lake Forest, Illinois*

Answer the question(s); be succinct, to the point and thoughtful; remember the rules of the English language; and, above all, be yourself. Those are my words of advice to students who ask about college essays. It sounds simple, and it should be, but admissions officers are always taken aback, in fact, shocked by what is sometimes presented to them. We will get pieces of work that seem to say, "I don't care about your institution; I don't want to attend and won't even if you admit me." We don't admit them and assume that makes them happy.

All of us are not equally blessed in terms of our writing style, articulateness, or persuasive powers but there is no reason each individual cannot communicate correctly. Admissions officers don't expect every 17 or 18 year old to be a budding Hemingway or Mark Twain. On the other hand, we do expect students to be able to write coherently, to demonstrate a knowledge of the rules of grammar, structure and syntax, to be able to carry on an argument, and to make a declarative statement. Admissions officers love to ask "why" after "what." For example: What subjects interest you? Why? In what courses have you done well (or poorly)? Why? What course has had a particularly strong influence on you? Why?

Think about it for a moment. These are natural questions to ask of someone planning to go to college. In just the same manner, aren't many of the "essay" questions on college applications natural questions to ask someone planning to go to college?

*Robert A. Sortland*
*College Counselor*
*John Burroughs School*
*St. Louis, Missouri*

My guess is that most applicants to colleges that require an essay believe that it is an obstacle (trap) strategically placed to keep them out of those particular colleges. I hate to say it, but I'm afraid that there may be a few college admissions officers who see the essay in the same light, although universally they tell kids that it should be seen as an opportunity—which it is.

The college application and supporting documents present essentially a two-dimensional teenager; the essay can give a perceptive reader at least a glimpse of a third dimension. A thoughtful, well-written essay certainly benefits both the candidate and admissions officers as the latter try to identify those applicants they think will add most to a freshman class. The essay, therefore, has utilitarian value for both the college and the candidate.

But I would argue that its **greater value** has to do with its writing, rather than with its audience. Approval gratifies, to be sure; thinking and presenting one's thinking as well as one can, not only gratifies, it stimulates, it induces growth, it educates. Now there's a novel thought for the senior year in high school! Because it has utility—or perhaps more importantly, because seniors believe it has utility—the college essay, probably more than most classroom assignments, is taken seriously. And it is likely to elicit an honest response, simply because the audience ("two or three admissions officers") is unknown. It is also more likely to be carefully edited and proofread—it should, after all, represent the best the student has to offer. Finally, and most essentially, the college application essay is by its very nature and timing an introspective exercise. The **process** of choosing a college is, I believe, more important than the eventual "**product**"; the essay provides an opportunity not only to present oneself accurately and positively, it also provides an opportunity for growth."

*Diane Haarman*
*Counselor*
*Nashoba Regional High School*
*Bolton, Massachusetts*

I believe that applying to college is one of the most powerful rites of passage in American society today. It is a time to take stock of where an individual has been and where he is headed—and why he is headed there. It is a time to reap what has been sown. The process of writing the college essay requires each applicant to find a shape and significance in seventeen or eighteen years of experience. It demands reflection and honest self-appraisal. When taken seriously, when grappled with ruthlessly and honestly, it is an enormously productive and powerful undertaking. The great college essay captures the very essence and soul of the applicant; it is always rather miraculous to read because it is, indeed, a window into the mind and soul of the individual. Great essays always have passion. So, what is problematic about this powerful experience? What troubles me as a counselor? Well . . .

Perhaps most significantly, it is incredibly difficult to write such an essay and write it well. I find that there is enormous misunderstanding about what an essay should be and how colleges use essays to make admissions decisions. This needs to be better delineated in the application packet!

Without a great deal of guidance and dialogue, even very bright students produce first draft essays that are boring, rather pedestrian and NOT particularly reflective or revealing. Extremely bright students often produce excruciatingly intellectual essays that reveal that they are, indeed, BRIGHT (which is obvious from their numbers) but their individual qualities and personalities do not shine through at all. These students often don't like their essays either, but they aren't sure how to fix them. They play it safe because they equate passion and self-revelation with bragging and excuse-making and are loathe to do either.

When I work with my seniors, I tell them that a great college application package is like a great piece of music. It consists of a theme and many variations. The essay is the primary theme and can ONLY be stated by the student. *Stated in the student's own words, it is the passionate expression of who he is and what he cares about.* It must be focused; it must be a distillation of what he cares about most deeply. If the essay works, the reader should finish it and know something essential and important about the applicant, just as if they had chatted about an important issue or situation for a little while.

My seniors and I "talk them out." (That works best!) They sometimes cry. They sometimes exclaim that they will never forget certain experiences. But I can honestly say that they almost always remark that writing the essay was worthwhile. I will never forget the great essays that they have written. I will never forget their struggles. And neither will they. Whether the decision is admit, reject, or wait list, seniors remember the struggle with the essay. It is a significant piece of the admissions process and an even more significant step toward adulthood.

*Dick Tobin*
*Counselor*
*Green Hills School*
*Ann Arbor, Michigan*

As I think about kids writing application essays, I find that I'm not seriously bothered by any significant aspect of the process. It goes almost without saying that it's legitimate for colleges to ask students to do this. Certainly they need to get some sense of writing competence; and although reading an essay is not the means most of us would choose to "get to know" another person, given the inherent limitations of interviewing, it's hard to know what other device colleges could dream up for the purpose.

I encourage kids to see essay questions as opportunities rather than as hurdles. Assuming that they are applying to a school that actually is interested in their ideas and personality (thus leaving aside places that are focused primarily on the numbers), this is their chance to let the institution know something important and true about them. I tell students that so long as they write on something they care about, and address it candidly and with some depth, their essay will almost inevitably have impact. It's for this reason that I'm not especially bothered by the gist of particular questions.

Of course, it's not always easy to get kids to do that. They may try to imagine the audience for which they're writing, and lose their own authentic voice accordingly; or become stiffly formal, or attempt humor that is not natural to them and falls flat, or be tentative rather than relaxed and clear. Around here it does take a good deal of cajolery, patience, support, and encouragement to get kids to write freely and confidently. Absent the kind of guidance we try to offer here, the potential for young people to slide into the kinds of ill-advised approaches mentioned above, and thus to write exactly the opposite of the essays admission officials are interested in reading, seems great. One conclusion to draw, and I'm sure it's hardly original with me, is that in the section of the application that asks for essay responses, some relaxing encouraging words as to "what we really want" might be offered—something along the lines of, "These questions are intended simply to give you a focus for your thoughts. While we do want you to respond to the intent of the question(s), feel free to shape your response as seems appropriate to you. Write a thoughtful, well-crafted, corrected essay—but be confident that we really want to know what you think!"

I think that colleges which ask for or allow the submission of a "graded paper" have a good idea. Though some high schools require more regular and varied writing than others, the fact is that there are a lot of kids who are already being asked to write papers which are similar to those being written at the colleges. If one of the major reasons for soliciting application essays is to determine the student's potential for handling college writing assignments, as it certainly must be, a similar paper written in high school could provide a good indicator. It also seems to me that, if students have had the chance to take an expository writing or composition class of some kind, the "incidental" work they've produced—a sketch, an opinion piece, a personal memory— might well be a valuable submission to the college.

And I wouldn't worry a lot about the integrity of such products. Papers produced for class assignments may, of course, have gone through any number of drafts, but if the teacher has handled the process appropriately the final product will have remained the student's own work. Given the proliferation of writing help centers on college campuses, the products that college students themselves are handing in are often the result of several drafts, with the intercession at important points of a student or other writing advisor. And of course published work done by college staff members or writers-at-large regularly receives significant editorial assistance.

These comments lead me to mention "help" on the essay written specifically for the application. The issue of what degree of assistance—by a college advisor, teacher, parent, peer—is acceptable, is complicated, and certainly appropriate limits are regularly abused. It has occurred to me in the past, however, that those who insist that the writing a student submits to a college must be kept completely pristine, untouched, as it were, by human suggestions, ignore the manner in which most good writing is produced. After some years of trying to work out for myself what it's legitimate for me to do when a student asks for my input on an essay (and having begun, long ago, with the assumption that I should keep my hands *entirely* off), I've concluded several things: (1) It's fine for me to act as a sounding board (to wit: "I see where you're heading here, but I'm not too clear on the second paragraph. Maybe you should give that more thought."); (2) I can provide suggestions about organization; and (3) I even feel okay about circling spelling/mechanical errors (though I might get some real debate on that point). The whole matter comes down to the wisdom and judgement of the advisor involved. Unquestionably, writing submitted must be the student's own work. Anyone who helps the student to "enhance" his or her writing to the point where it does not accurately represent the student's real ability is doing a disservice both to the institution to which the student is applying and to the young person. But I do think it's appropriate for an advisor to assist the student in submitting the best writing of which the student is capable.

*Kathlynn C. Ciompi*
*Director*
*College Counselor*
*The Baylor School*
*Chattanooga, Tennessee*

It is fun to have been on both sides of the desk from which vantage points the importance of the essay to personalize the application and to provide a writing sample cannot be underestimated.

From a college admissions perspective, I always appreciated those essays where the student incorporated some humor. Not everyone can use humor effectively in writing, but if one has this talent, weary admissions officers really appreciate the break from super serious topics, particularly when applications are being read late into the night.

From the high school side, I see the students really agonizing about what to say in the essay and how to write it. Considering the time and energy that go into the well-written ones, I am so pleased (and the students are really impressed) when a college admissions officer writes to compliment the student on his or her essay. Feedback of this type is so constructive and very much appreciated. It conveys the message that good writing is important, and that someone really is reading those essays in the admissions office.

*Paul Abbott*
*Director of College Counseling*
*South Kent (Connecticut) School*

The essay. Where to begin? I have never felt comfortable with the notion it was to be a writing sample. English teachers, Daddy's secretary, and spelling checkers, all have made the essay something other than an individual's own work. There is irony here. We suggest that a student do everything, but all professional writers work with editors. What message are we trying to send?

I get annoyed with college folk who say "Catch my attention." "Please not another essay on my most forgettable experience." If the purpose of the essay is to wake up bored admissions counselors reading 75 folders a day, it should be dropped at once. Readers who reject the efforts made by frightened young men and women to please them should get out of the business.

Is there a purpose for the essay requirement? I believe it can add useful information that cannot be gotten in any other manner. A good essay about working as a short order cook in a local diner could tell much about values. A perceptive analysis about a trip to a Third World nation would flesh out a stated interest in social work. A discussion about helping a retarded younger brother prepare for the Special Olympics would reveal character. An admission counselor might very well read 50 essays on "My most unforgettable experience," but let's remember that we are talking about fifty different kids.

An essay that asks for clarification of personal values and goals may be pompously written and a bit over done, yet incredibly genuine. They must be read for what they mean to the writer. If what is said seems real and in step with the rest of the candidate's record, the essay is valid.

Should we require them? Yes. We do need to become more imaginative readers, however, and remember the pressure and circumstances the author is working through. The kids want to please, but they do not want to be used. A cynical response by a reader undoes everything.

*William M. Hartog*
*Director of Admissions and Financial Aid*
*Washington and Lee University*
*Lexington, Virginia*

There has been much written and said about the importance of the essay in the college admissions process, and frequently I find myself in disagreement. To be sure, colleges which require essays employ admissions committees which will spend countless hours reading them. And I will concede that a committee's perception of a candidate can at times be reinforced by an essay's construction and content. To suggest as some do, however, that decisions routinely turn on essays is preposterous. What gets the overwhelming majority of young people into the college of their choice is an excellent academic record, including program of study, grades, rank in class if available, and standardized test results. All other factors are simply icing on the cake.

*Nicky Carpenter*
*Educational Consultant*
*Wayzata, Minnesota*

The college essays are indeed controversial these days for a lot of reasons. Who really writes them? Is it really only the student? If so, the exercise is well worth it because it causes the student to consider carefully where he/she is going to apply. The student's time-line is limited so they can't just fire off a bunch of applications with essays the way they would fill in the blanks. They must invest something of themselves in each application and to do that with limited time they are making a commitment. Of course it gives the admission committee an opportunity to see the student's ability to organize and indeed, through the essay, the student's level of maturity. We all know it's much more fun if the topic of the essay brings forth something substantial, but that's secondary to my way of thinking. Some students are more creative than others and that's just a fact of life. However, every student can learn how to write a well put together essay and this is what I think is most important. If they lack basic language skills they will benefit from a specific college environment more than another.

The essay loses all importance when it is heavily critiqued by a teacher, talented friend, or a presumably well-meaning consultant. What about the disadvantaged student? I don't care whether they are disabled in some way or culturally or racially less privileged or grew up in a school system in which they didn't have the opportunities to learn and practice writing skills. Filling in the blanks will never provide the admission committee the opportunity to see into the qualities of that applicant. What a waste of the many talents teenagers have and how too bad to maybe deprive X college and its students of potential racial, cultural, and social diversity. There is always something worthwhile to say.

Of course, requiring essays is a luxury which only colleges with a finite applicant group can enjoy. It would not be possible in large public institutions. Then again, a salvo toward the critics who decry the emphasis on test scores. Well, how would they want decisions to be made? If it's solely on grades, they'll complain that the disadvantaged students never had the opportunity to excel because of something wrong in his environment. It must be a no-win situation.''

*Patricia B. Hitz Taylor*
*Guidance Counselor*
*Bronxville (New York) High School*

I view the essay as one of the few opportunities for a candidate to take on their own personality. I describe the essay as a "window" to be used in the process. This is the student's opportunity to open the curtains and let the admissions office see the inside; or, through a poorly written essay, the student can keep their curtains half-drawn and their personality, their passions and their interests hidden. The analogy has been simple enough for all to grasp. I laughed with one parent who came in after the essay was submitted and told me that she was afraid her son not only opened the curtains but also, by telling too many family stories, had left open all the windows.

My point in all of this is that we all know the basic truths of length, of being grammatically correct and all of those easier to discuss issues. The truth, from my limited perspective, is that the essay needs to supply the "meat," the answers to the unanswered transcript questions. Personal passions, personal gains and tenacity are the sparks that allow others to gain new perspective on a student's application. The sparks coming from the essay.

*Thekla Shackelford*
*Educational Consultant*
*Gahanna, Ohio*

The essay is our favorite part of the admissions process. The essay requirement enables us to get inside the head and heart of each student. It is an exposition, under some pressure, of a topic the student usually knows well—herself or himself. In getting to know students and their parents, we ask probing questions. More often than not, we get candid responses. It is not, however, until a student begins to face the threat of exposing himself/herself on paper that true colors emerge.

No part of the admissions process seems quite so concrete as the essay. Nowhere else is the student so exposed or so personally vulnerable. The mystery or magic of the essay begins to unfold as we help students search for a topic. It gives us a chance to know them creatively and intellectually. The thought processes they use as they determine the poignant or important moments that have impacted their lives reveal their values, sensitivities, learning styles, and views of the world and fellow human beings. As we work through the process, students increasingly reveal strengths and weaknesses—i.e., are they willing to take criticism? How hard are they willing to work to achieve a superior product? What is the state of their egos, self-confidence, self-knowledge, ability to articulate a point of view, creativity, and self-expression?

A most rewarding experience is when a student after five or six attempts reaches deep into himself and finds a topic so absorbing that the essay flows comfortably and, in turn, allows the reader to know more than the statistics presented on the application. Some of our most precious moments over the past 15 years have been when we see pride on a student's face when he at last feels that he has written well. Heartening, too, is the student who might have limited academic ability but comes alive through his writing. Disheartening is the 4.0 student with 1400 Board scores who is so inhibited he cannot express himself through the essay.

*Carol Gill*
*Educational Consultant*
*Dobbs Ferry, New York*

I do think the essay is important in a special way. We all know that colleges have become overly concerned with their placements in Barron's selective categories, so that test scores, GPA, class rank are more significant than ever. As personal interviews become a thing of the past, the personal essay gives applicants the only real opportunity to present themselves to the admissions committee. It also should be a way to express a deep commitment to someone or something, to display a great sense of humor or a vivid intellectual curiosity or imagination.

*Jane McLure*
*Educational Consultant*
*San Francisco, California*

I think colleges invite students to "cheat" on their application essays when they ask questions which are beyond the range of perception, understanding or knowledge of most 17-year-olds. One college asked students to write an essay on how growing up in their communities helped shape their attitudes toward racism, sexism, and prejudice. Surely, these attitudes are not completely formed before a student goes off to college, when their experiences and depth of understanding are so limited.

Colleges should ask questions which are appropriate for the intellectual, social, emotional, and moral development of adolescents, since that is what most college applicants are.

# Appendix

## ADVISORIES

**Positive**

- Brevity is a virtue.

- Improve your vocabulary.

- Allow yourself plenty of time for writing.

- Be yourself.

- Write as you would speak—in conversational terms.

- Always write from an outline.

- Learn the difference between an adverb and an adjective.

- Strive to summarize. You will, at all times, command attention with the short version.

- Learn to be clear and concise.

- Learn the difference between *few* and *less.*

- Learn the difference between *like* and *as.*

- Read and read and read some more.

- Make absolutely certain that you proofread your work.

- Familiarize yourself with the subjunctive:
  (1) pure supposition—If I *were* king (not If I was king)
  (2) after verbs of wishing—I wish she *were* here (not I wish she was here).

*Negative*
- Never end a sentence with a preposition.

- Strip the following from your vocabulary:
  *like*
  *I mean*
  *ya know*
  *right?.*

- Never assume anything.

- Do not mix your verb tenses.

- Avoid double negatives.

- Avoid double comparatives.

- Do not expect to accomplish important writing in one sitting.

- Avoid the phrase *a lot of.*

- Avoid run-on sentences.

# Afterword

*Communicating Clearly*

Communication is a very integral part of our daily lives. What we say or write and how we say or write it is really a developmental measure of our level of intelligence.

Ron Potier of Elizabethtown College has a keen eye for humor. He submitted the following as a humorous example of something coming out the way it was not intended.

An essay I read several years ago was addressing the problem of apathy at the student's high school. The student's concerns were deep and the words impassioned. She made a strong case for better student and teacher involvement in the life of the school and warned that the issues needed to be addressed promptly. In closing her essay, she summed it all up by writing, "We must stop sitting on our hands watching the future slip through our fingers."

WITHDRAWN